PEACE COUNTRY

PEACE COUNTRY

Pedro Chamale

PLAYWRIGHTS CANADA PRESS
Toronto

Jacket art by Kiana Hipolito
Author photo by Brandon Hart Photography

Playwrights Canada Press
202-269 Richmond St. W., Toronto, ON M5V 1X1
416.703.0013 | info@playwrightscanada.com | www.playwrightscanada.com

LIBRARY AND ARCHIVES CANADA CATALOGUING IN PUBLICATION
Title: Peace country / Pedro Chamale.
Names: Chamale, Pedro, author.
Description: First edition.
Identifiers: Canadiana (print) 20240409965 | Canadiana (ebook) 20240410025
    | ISBN 9780369105189 (softcover) | ISBN 9780369105196 (PDF)
    | ISBN 9780369105202 (EPUB)
Subjects: LCGFT: Drama.
Classification: LCC PS8605.H3388 P43 2024 | DDC C812/.6—dc23

Playwrights Canada Press staff work across Turtle Island, on Treaty 7, Treaty 13, and Treaty 20 territories, which are the current and ancestral homes of the Anishinaabe Nations (Ojibwe / Chippewa, Odawa, Potawatomi, Algonquin, Saulteaux, Nipissing, and Mississauga / Michi Saagiig), the Blackfoot Confederacy (Kainai, Piikani, and Siksika), néhiyaw, Sioux, Stoney Nakoda, Tsuut'ina, Wendat, and members of the Haudenosaunee Confederacy (Mohawk, Oneida, Onondaga, Cayuga, Seneca, and Tuscarora), as well as Metis and Inuit peoples. It always was and always will be Indigenous land.

We acknowledge the financial support of the Canada Council for the Arts, the Ontario Arts Council (OAC), Ontario Creates, the Government of Ontario, and the Government of Canada for our publishing activities.

For my dad, Big Pedro.

SEARCHING FOR
PEACE COUNTRY
Heidi Taylor

In our early *Peace Country* meetings, Pedro played me recordings he had made with family members in Chetwynd. We met outside on my back deck in the midst of the pandemic lockdowns. We shared stories about our respective times in more or less remote places as young people. He has taken the heart and soul of those recordings and his stories and made them into this play.

Since those meetings, Pedro produced a workshop production, a world premiere, and two children. Meanwhile the experience of fire in BC's north transformed, growing exponentially in its scale and impact on communities. These changes—a new generation arriving and real fires taking the place of an imagined one—brought an urgency not only to the play, but to the creative team's search for hope.

Hope arrived in the warm relationships that Pedro rekindled in Chetwynd as he researched the workshop draft and the premiere rewrite. It emerged in Indigenous-led climate action, including the Salish Fire Keepers Society and the Gathering Voices initiative. We held on to it to bear witness when a team member recounted her experience of driving away from the 2016 Fort McMurray fire, hometown blazing in her rearview mirror, as part of the largest evacuation in Alberta history. Hope was built one line at a time as Pedro knit two selves together, north and south, with new understandings of both world views.

As Pedro's dramaturg, I was aware of my distance to the material. But I also brought parallel experiences from living in Edmonton and Thunder Bay—a few degrees latitude south of Chetwynd, but with translatable versions of teenage bush parties, parking-lot hangouts, and suspicion of the south. Our Millennial and Gen X histories provided a kind of cultural research for cast members who then added their own unique lenses, contributing essential insights into the play's dramaturgy.

Pedro captures the contradictions inherent in the northern community he grew up in, but also in the southern response to the climate emergency when it's transplanted to a northern context. These characters inhabit a reality where some people move back and forth, switching dialects as they cross Highway 16, and others choose a location not only to live in but to fight for. He allows the people who he knows—north and south—to speak through these characters. To grapple. To love and disappoint each other. And to live in the unknown.

I remember the moment when Pedro changed a line of Melissa's from "hard times are coming for us" to "hard times are here for us." There was a collective swallow in the room. Hard times aren't new, but they are confronting people across geographic and class differences with a ferocity that's breathtaking. And in places where you have to rely on your neighbour, whether you agree with them or not, we're receiving an education in the possibilities and limits of community solidarity. Reading *Peace Country* is a chance to witness the evolution of a group of friends and their individual routes to action. And, perhaps, to find our own sources of hope.

Heidi Taylor is a dramaturg based on the traditional, stolen, and occupied territories of the xʷməθkwəy̓əm (Musqueam), Skwxwú7mesh (Squamish), and səl̓ílwətaɬ (Tsleil-Waututh) Nations. She is omnivorous in her theatrical tastes, developing performances from first idea through production for sited, text-based, community-engaged, and solo works. She has dramaturged over twenty world premieres, including Pedro Chamale's Peace Country, *Derek Chan's* Happy Valley, *Carmen Aguirre's* Anywhere But Here, *and Tetsuro Shigematsu's* Empire of the Son. *She served as Artistic & Executive Director of Playwrights Theatre Centre from 2012 until 2024.*

PREFACE

Welcome to Peace Country

This play is the third in a trilogy called my Northern Lights trilogy, which is inspired by my life, my family, and living in Canada's North. I knew that I wanted to conclude the trilogy by featuring my hometown. I wanted the characters to be based on the folks who live there and highlight the reality of what it's like to survive in small towns. Too many times have I seen plays and movies portray small towns as idyllic backdrops for the big-city protagonist to have their life-changing epiphanies. Knowing that this work was to be staged in "the big city" I wanted to bring these kind, smart, and complicated people that I grew up with onto a city stage. To try and make audiences love them as much as I do. But while I knew who was to populate this play, I had no clue as to what the hell it would be about.

While smashing my head against a wall and promising my (at the time) co-artistic director at rice & beans drafts that didn't exist, I took part in The Only Animal production of *Slime*. What an incredibly fortuitous opportunity that was. Not only did it let me sink my teeth into a wonderful play that pondered our role in this global crisis, they challenged the cast to come up with climate pieces of our own. What I dreamed up was not *Peace Country* but a half dozen ideas yelling at people for not being more scared of our collective future. I was angry at how severe the damage that has been done and frustrated by my perceived inability to make any significant change being in the world of theatre. Small indie theatre to be exact. That's when I knew what *Peace Country* had to be about.

While I was in those early conceptual stages of imagining what kind of play could spark action in both suburban city dwellers and rural residents, I received word that a childhood friend and fellow high school theatre nerd, Sean McGarry, died in an avalanche. He was an experienced backcountry sledder, a father, and dear friend to many but was gone in an instant. In my own journey to process this loss I came across research stating how the change in our climate has led to an increase in the frequency of avalanches outside of the season. This then led to a concept of what *Peace Country* was to be at first. It would snow indoors and we would (or attempt to) recreate the northern lights inside of a theatre. Bring some of that Northern magic from my hometown to the south, where home is now.

After our workshop production in 2022, I realized something wasn't working. I wanted to honour my friend with an avalanche and highlight our drastically changing climate with the immediate threat of being buried. However, it turned out to be too passive. I also needed some dedicated writing time since most of the workshop production was written with my newborn son sleeping on my chest. Or squeezed between his 4 a.m. feed and my 8 a.m. deadline for new pages before rehearsal.

While attending the National Playwrights Retreat at the Caravan Farm, begging my brain to figure out what was needed, I recalled the last time I had been on the Farm. When Derek Chan and I were asked to come up and create a land walk. As we drove the Coquihalla Highway, smoke blanketed the scenery. We arrived to be told that the area was on evacuation alert and to be ready to flee if necessary. One evening while having dinner outside, it began to snow on us as we chatted. It was snowing ash. A forest fire was just over the hill. A forest fire was what was needed in *Peace Country*.

Forest fires have become synonymous with summer nowadays; becoming a poster child for the climate crisis. Especially for those of us here on the west coast. I reworked almost the entirety of *Peace Country* to fit this new natural disaster. I mused about Tumbler Ridge, BC burning to the ground only to seemingly have predicted the future because a month later Tumbler would be evacuated due to forest fires. As we entered rehearsals in the fall, tears stung my eyes as we spoke about how timely this play was. Yet again the area from my childhood was in danger. The Donnie Creek wildfire, north of Fort St. John, BC, the largest in the province's history, was raging.

Even as I write this preface, residents of Fort Nelson, BC have been put on evaluation notice. My hometown of Chetwynd has a fire blazing fourteen kilometres south of it.

This isn't some speculative fiction about what might happen if we don't fix our ways. I may have chosen to set it a few years in the future but this is happening right now. This play may soon become a historical one. A window to when we refused to work across political lines and allowed the world to burn around us. I can only hope that *Peace Country* can play a small part in calling folks to action, to demand real change from our governments. Real consequences for the biggest contributors to climate change. But that will only happen if we listen to each other.

Peace Country was first presented as a workshop production by rice & beans theatre in partnership with Playwrights Theatre Centre at the Shadbolt Centre for the Arts from April 27 to 30, 2022, with the following cast and creative team:

Greg: Garvin Chan
Alicia: Sofía Rodríguez
Melissa: Sara Vickruck
Julia: Montserrat Videla
Candice: Kaitlyn Yott

Director: Pedro Chamale
Assistant Director: María Escolán
Dramaturg: Heidi Taylor
Set/Props Designer: Kimira Reddy
Video Designer: Vanka Salim
Lighting Designer: Jessica Han
Costume Designer: Michelle Thorne
Sound Designer: Cindy Kao
Associate Sound Designer: Alistair Wallace
Stage Manager: Koh Lauren Quan
Assistant Stage Manager: Mariana Munoz
Production Manager: Jamie Sweeney
Producer: Heather Barr

The play received its world premiere at the Firehall Arts Centre, October 12 to 22, 2023, in a production by rice & beans theatre, developed in association with Playwrights Theatre Centre, in association with Vancouver Asian Canadian Theatre and created with support from the Push International Performing Arts Festival, and developed in part through the 2023 National Playwrights Retreat at the Caravan Farm. It featured the following cast and creative team:

Alicia: Sofía Rodríguez
Julia: Manuela Sosa
Melissa: Sara Vickruck
Greg: Angus Yam
Candice: Kaitlyn Yott

Director: Pedro Chamale
Dramaturg: Heidi Taylor
Costume Designer: Michelle Thorne
Lighting Designer: Jonathan Kim
Sound Designer: Cindy Kao
Set and Props Designer: Kimira Reddy
Set and Props Design Assistant: Monica Emme
Video Designer: Andie Lloyd
Video Design Assistant: June Hsu
Stage Manager: Julia Lank
Technical Director: Jack Goodison
Production Manager: Kayleigh Sandomirsky
Producer: Heather Barr

CHARACTERS

CANDICE: The owner of the Muffin Break. Grew up on the reserve outside town.

JULIA: A newly elected MLA for a Vancouver riding, she and Candice were childhood best friends. Canadian-born kid of the only Guatemalan immigrants in town.

ALICIA: Owner of a full-service civil construction and logging contracting business. Julia's sister. She is older by two years and moved back home after dropping out of college. Born in Guatemala, raised in Canada.

GREG: Town councillor and volunteer firefighter. He took over the Chinese restaurant in town when his immigrant parents retired. Canadian-born kid of the only Hong Kong immigrants in town.

MELISSA: Works at the mill and volunteers at the Pride Society. Moved to town at age ten and went away to university.

All of these characters grew up together, within a few blocks of each other. They were all born and raised here except for Melissa who moved to town in elementary school. They were friends, they were as close as family.

NOTES

All effort should be made to cast these characters the way I have written them with regard to their cultural background. If that cannot be done then please move on to another IBPOC person.

There are many swear words throughout the text. For most folks that would mean putting emphasis on those words, but for these characters that is not the case. They do not indicate anger, conflict, or high levels of emotion. The swear words are just part of their everyday speech. Overemphasizing these words will disrupt the rhythms and make the stakes too high when that is not intended.

The characters that live full-time in the Peace should have a bit of a lilt to their speech. Not a stereotypical Canadian or Maritime accent, but more of rural small town western Canada sound. You can hear it in the elongation of "o" or "ah" sounds or placing them farther back in the mouth. There is also a slightly harder "r" sound as well. To get a better sense of it, look up "Albertan Accent." Adult Julia's dialect shift to a more standard Lower Mainland BC is one way the differences between the characters is expressed.

Translated text in square brackets [ ] is there to provide context for non-Spanish speaking people. It's not to be read after the Spanish. Either the Spanish or English can be read depending on the ability of the actor.

SETTING

A small town nestled in the northeastern area of British Columbia known as the Peace River Regional District, unceded, ancestral, and traditional territories of the Treaty 8 Nations, including Sikanni, Slavey, Beaver (Dunne-za), Cree, and Saulteau. In that town there are all the things you would expect. One stoplight, one grocery store, and one gas station. The play takes place in and around a local coffee/muffin shop called Muffin Break, on the trails, and in the bush. The set needs to convey small town and sparsely populated. This is a town with fewer than three thousand inhabitants. The set should allow for the fluidity of memory to flow and the smashing of timelines.

TIME PERIODS

Present day, a night in their teens, childhood.

ACT ONE

SCENE 1: ELECTION NIGHT

We see four people hanging out at Muffin Break, a place they have frequented since they were kids. There are bottles of beer strewn across the space. It is one of the last franchises of Muffin Break that once dotted towns all over British Columbia. You could find the same set-up in any Muffin Break, but since the main company went under, the uniformity has not been strictly enforced. It has been an institution of this small town for years. It is election night in British Columbia, normally not an event to gather for in this town. They are playing crib.

GREG: Whose crib is it?

MELISSA: Mine.

They throw cards to the crib.

Cut the deck.

ALICIA: When are we gunna know the results?

MELISSA: When the polls close. Two for Johnny.

ALICIA: And that is?

CANDICE: Polls close at eight. Then early results should come in soon after.

ALICIA: Ugh, I'm going to need another drink then.

CANDICE: I ain't stopping ya.

MELISSA: Don't think ya could if ya tried.

CANDICE: Yah right, you might be a pushover, Melissa, but I'm tough as steel!

ALICIA: I could snap you in two with my pinky.

CANDICE: Oh yah? Why don't you close that bullshitting mouth of yours and go get your drink already.

ALICIA goes and gets a drink.

GREG: You wanna grab me one too while you're up, Al?

ALICIA: Fuck you, Greg.

GREG: Candice, thanks for hosting. Four.

CANDICE: Ten. No prob. One of the perks of being the owner here. I can close up for my own private functions.

MELISSA: Ya shoulda stayed open tonight. We coulda had a proper election party!

CANDICE: Nah, are you kidding me? I wouldn't want to clean up dat mess.

ALICIA: You're messier than anyone else I know in town. Twenty-four.

CANDICE: Fuck you!

MELISSA: Thirty-one for two. Do you think Jules will win?

CANDICE: Nice.

GREG: Seven.

CANDICE: Fifteen for two.

ALICIA: Fuck you. Twenty-three for two.

GREG: It's Jules, she has a horseshoe up her ass, she'll win. Not sure about her party though, they've only been around for a hot minute. Might pick up a few seats in Vancouver but probably not much more'n that.

ALICIA: Did they even run a candidate up here?

MELISSA: They did! Some goober from Prince. Twenty-nine.

GREG: *(laughing)* Goober?

MELISSA: Yah, goober. She was smart and was saying all the party jargon. But it did just seem like they found anyone up here to run for them.

CANDICE: Everyone round here just votes for who won last time.

GREG: Speak for yourself.

CANDICE: Oh really, then who did you vote for, G?

GREG: Well if you must know, our honourable incumbent.

CANDICE: See! Just toeing the company line.

GREG: His platform aligned well with my concerns.

CANDICE: Sure it did.

GREG: Go.

CANDICE: You should have run, G. Thirty.

ALICIA: Go.

MELISSA: Go.

CANDICE: Thirty-one for four.

GREG: Fuck off! I'm doing enough already in this town. Don't need to also work outta Victoria half the year.

The sound of the TV comes back in. We hear the news anchor.

ANCHOR: . . . one for the record books. With all pre-election polls show-ing less than a point difference in the NDP and BC United Parties, the real variable here is the BCEA and their strong hold in voters aged 18-25. That demographic could decide who will form this province's next govern-ment. To talk about what our leadership could look like after the polls close tonight, we are joined by CBC's election panel of experts . . .

The voices are turned down by ALICIA.

ALICIA: Why are elections so boring? Seven.

CANDICE: What do you want?

ALICIA: I dunno, maybe something like a halftime show.

MELISSA: Seriously? Sixteen.

GREG: Twenty-four for three.

CANDICE: Go.

ALICIA: Yah, or they could throw a big public concert at the Olympic torch. Have some local band just rock out once the polls close. Go.

CANDICE: You would think you'd be plenty interested what with yur little sis running and all.

MELISSA: Yah, Al. It's a big deal Jules's one of the youngest to run. Twenty-nine.

ALICIA: I'm happy for her, I hope she wins but I'm not too excited for that party of hers.

GREG: That's two of us. Four.

MELISSA: What? They sound great! Pro-environment with a focus on a Just Transition.

ALICIA: What the fuck does that even mean? Taking jobs from folks up here? One for last go.

CANDICE: No, you idiot. It's the opposite. You know Eric who up and quit on you last week?

ALICIA: Ugh don't fuckin' remind me. I'm down one of my best guys.

CANDICE: He signed up for one of them retraining programs. Green energy needs trades people too.

MELISSA: Yah, 'cept Eric's gotta fuckin' shell out the cash himself.

ALICIA: Why isn't the province ponying up?

GREG: 'Cause their wallets are puckered tighter than their assholes.

CANDICE: Yah, but the BCEA plan tah fund folks who wanna transition industries!

GREG: Sure, but where the fuck is that cash gunna come from? Huh? It's gunna come from us. From our tax dollars, all to just give big oil the middle finger.

CANDICE: More like they're going to make sure companies like Suncor cough up the dough for the training centres.

GREG: Oh so now you want their money but not their jobs?

CANDICE: Fucking rights. They helped fuck up this planet more'n anyone so why shouldn't they fork over the money tah fix it.

MELISSA: Amen!

ALICIA: Don't you work for the sawmill?

MELISSA: It's just to pay the bills. I'm working on bigger things.

ALICIA: Oh sure, sure. Big plans in the works for the past, what? Ten years?

MELISSA: Fuck off!

GREG: Better get those plans rolling now, Mel. Who knows how long West Fraser's gunna be open. They might follow suit just like Canfor did if the BCEA is in charge.

CANDICE: Greg, look, the BCEA is the only party that has the fucking nuts to actually take these industries to task. There's gunna be collateral damage.

ALICIA: So we're just supposed to be cool with being collateral damage?

CANDICE: Yur gunna be fine, Al.

ALICIA: Who do you think I get most of my contracts from, Candice?

GREG: Who cares, they're not gunna be any different.

CANDICE: Fuck you, ya could at least gave them a chance to see if they had any follow through. We don't have the time to pussyfoot around the climate issue with the same fucking leadership that got us here in the first place. I'm fine for energy companies and contractors to stay in the province Alicia, if they can fuckin' adapt.

GREG: All parties have an environmental message. Clean energy, green energy, diversifying our energy portfolio. Let's cut those emissions down while ramping up our industry market shares.

CANDICE: Who cares what they need to be told to get on board, as long as they do.

GREG: I do! And so does the mayor and the rest of town council!

CANDICE: Those cowards? They just care about what's going to get them a photo in the *Coffee Talk*.

GREG: Doesn't matter, we're still the ones making decisions for the whole town. We have to figure how tah navigate all these "necessary" changes that Victoria punts out. Last week alone we had three motions for expedited approval for exploratory digs so these "green" mining folks can come look for their rare metals to put into all your recharge-ables. Green isn't always clean!

CANDICE: Real fuckin' original. You sound like every climate change denier I've ever met.

GREG: I never said I don't believe in climate change, you spaz. I know things are fucked up all over the place.

CANDICE: Who cares about all over the place. It's happening in our own backyard. I'm fucking praying we don't watch all the roads outta here get washed out again like last summer.

ALICIA: I mean I wouldn't really mind it. It was a great contract fixing up the roads after that mess.

MELISSA: Holy, don't try 'n sound so happy 'bout that, you vulture.

CANDICE: What we really need is all levels of government to work with the Indigenous leadership. Look at the native plant nursery?

A fuckin' shining example of how Indigenous practices can start turning the ship around.

GREG: And who do you think was the first person on council to ask what kinda help West Moberly and Saulteau needed for that, huh? Me!

CANDICE: Then why wouldn't you be excited about a party that has realistic plans?

GREG: All I'm concerned about this election is which party is going to fuck our little town over the least. I'd love to vote with my heart like you but as a town councillor I have to also think of what's best for our prospects. About which government is going to be easiest to work with in order to be heard, let alone actually be considered in the decision process.

CANDICE: I get that, Greg, but Victoria makes decisions with or without our input all the time.

MELISSA: Yah! What about the fucking Caribou Recovery Program? Fucking booted us out of our backcountry.

CANDICE: Your backcountry?

MELISSA: Candice, you know what I mean.

CANDICE: I'm fucking with you.

> *CANDICE goes to get beer.*

GREG: Exactly. The future of caribou was more important to the NDP than the impact on lives or future industry prospects.

CANDICE: I hear you, Greg. But there aren't going to be any fucking future prospects if there's no Earth.

GREG: Look, we're struggling enough to draw new business to town let alone keep what we got. What do you think's gunna happen once regulations get stricter?

MELISSA: I'm just as concerned as you about industry just up and leaving but if you look at what each party is promising, Jules's party is the only one who seems actually able to pull it off. They have plans on how to take care of us up here.

GREG: I never said that I don't see that. But that still doesn't mean that they'll care about any of us up here after the election. Promises and ideals mean nothing in the face of actually making a government work.

ALICIA: Has any party ever given a shit about us.

CANDICE: No. They only care about what we add to the province's GDP. Remember Site C.

MELISSA, GREG, and ALICIA groan in agreement. ALICIA has turned up the TV.

ANCHOR: It is now 8:15 p.m. and polls have closed. All parties are holding their breaths as results begin to trickle in. What was thought might be a three-way race in almost every riding is shaping up into a very different picture. Contrary to the NDP fears of vote-splitting that would give BC United an edge, it seems like there's been a wholesale move from NDP to BCEA, even beyond the expected demographic shift.

This next government may actually be decided by who can pick up more rural support tonight. Let's go over now and take a look at the Kootenay region to see how that area is shaping up.

ALICIA mutes the TV.

MELISSA: What about our riding?

GREG: Like our riding would ever flip.

CANDICE: At least voting for them shows they have support up here.

GREG: Sure for whatever that does. I need another drink. Whose turn is it to deal?

MELISSA: Yours.

GREG: Can someone shuffle for me?

CANDICE: Yup.

ALICIA: You know what, I really learned something tonight.

MELISSA: What?

ALICIA: I learned that you all take this so seriously.

GREG: Of course we do.

CANDICE: I can't believe you don't.

ALICIA: Why? Nothin' good comes of it, s'why I didn't vote.

They all look at ALICIA.

MELISSA: You didn't vote!?!

ALICIA: Nope.

MELISSA: But your sister's running for a seat.

ALICIA: Not like I live in her riding.

GREG: But you could have still voted for someone.

ALICIA: Why bother?

CANDICE: Because . . . because . . .

ALICIA: I never vote.

MELISSA: Why?!?!

ALICIA: At first it was 'cause I wasn't a citizen and couldn't. Then once I could, I didn't see the point.

> *They all look at* ALICIA. ALICIA, *unfazed once again, unmutes the* TV. *The sound of the election coverage theme song begins to play.*

Anyways, the results are coming in!

CANDICE: You are one of a kind, Al.

ALICIA: You betcha.

GREG: Deserves a drink.

MELISSA: Drinking game?

CANDICE: Hold on, I need another!

GREG: Rules?

MELISSA: Every time they say incumbent, drink!

CANDICE: When they say too close to call.

MELISSA: Good one.

GREG: When a riding flips!

CANDICE: Yes!

ALICIA: How about when Jules's party earns a seat?

MELISSA: Sure but since you didn't vote you have to drink when they mention voter turnout.

ALICIA: Can't be that much can it?

They all laugh. The TV sound is turned up.

ANCHOR: This is very exciting folks. Early results showed tight races across the province but the newly formed BC Environmental Alliance, or the BCEA, has taken a commanding lead in almost all of the ridings where they have run a candidate. Seems that this election the people of British Columbia are saying it's time to break the cycle of flipping between NDP and former Liberal party governments.

Let's take a look now at the race in Vancouver–Kensington. Even though it's been a long-time NDP stronghold, the BCEA chose to have one of their least experienced members run against the incumbent. Julia Jemenez started out as a fierce enviro-activist who turned MLA candidate. Early count had Jemenez ahead by a small margin, but that gap has been widening as more votes come in. I for one will be very interested to see what the voter turnout for this election will be and what kind of impact it has on the results.

CANDICE, GREG, & MELISSA: Drink, drink, drink!

ALICIA takes a big swig and punches CANDICE on the shoulder. The TV plays on.

SCENE 2: IGNITION

As the lights go down, we hear the rustling of trees, dry as tinder swaying to and fro. The sound of distant thunder is heard in the darkness. We hear rain starting to fall in its familiar pitter-patter, lightly drenching the leaves that have not had rain for some time. The ground, just as dry, drinks deeply but it is not enough.

The wind picks up and the swaying of the trees becomes more violent. The skies light up from a flash of lightning, all goes dark again. The thunder comes in five seconds after, signalling that the storm is about 1.3 km away. The wind picks up again. Maybe a tree falls as the rain has eroded some roots and the trees have lost so much to hold onto.

Another flash and the space lights up. The thunder quicker this time, signals the ever-closer bolts of lightning. More and more flashes split the skies and the thunder is right on top of us. We reach the peak of the storm and it passes over, pushed on by the high winds.

As we feel that we can take a breath once again, we hear it. Perhaps not certain at first but it's there. A crackle, a pop. The lighting has ignited the forest. We hear the fire build and we see the first strokes of light cover the dark canvas that is a forest at night. It continues to grow—for now, slowly. As the light builds it changes and morphs colours. Shadows dance across the stage.

SCENE 3: MELISSA

The dancing lights change into a kaleidoscope of colour that is the magic of the northern lights. They are both haunting and captivating. In the glow of the lights we see MELISSA outside.

MELISSA: They call this area of the province postcard country because everywhere you look it seems like it should be on a postcard. The quaint rolling foothills of the Rockies, sweeping forest, little towns blanketed in snow, and all sorts of wildlife roaming around. Scrawled on top would be "The Peace Country welcomes you." And welcome you it does, you'll never find friendlier people as far as I'm concerned, but what those postcards don't give you is any sense of what it's really like to live here.

What they don't show you are the shoulder months, when the roads are more dirt than anything else. When all that pristine white snow is brown and oil-stained, clinging to the wheel wells of 4x4 trucks until someone gives it a boot and it sluffs off.

It can be really tough. It can cost so much to survive here. And you don't really know it till you get out. Till you experience what living in the big city is like for the first time. What it's like to have amenities, art, or stores that are open past six. Or what it's like to be seen for who you truly are. Because as much as I love my friends here there was always something layered between us. I thought maybe it was 'cause I moved here in grade four and you just can't make up that history.

I didn't know I needed to escape this town until I got to university. I flourished. I came out halfway through my first year. Made up for the years I denied who I was. Like an Amish kid out on Rumspringa. Once I graduated, I found a great full-time job. Great crew. Great pay. It afforded me a decent life. I was happy, for the most part. Sometimes I'd have this nagging feeling. Like that feeling you get as you walk into a room and could swear you were looking for something but can't for the life of you remember. But that was only sometimes.

I had a girlfriend I loved. We started planning for a future, a life together. Talked about moving in with each other. Would it be mine or hers. Biggest fight in our whole relationship. I had the better location but she was in a co-op so rent was amazing. But on my way home from work one day, at the corner of Broadway and Main, I paused. I could hear the beep beep beep beep from the crossing light, but I just stood there. I watched people get on and off the 99. I must have stood there for an hour. Just watching people. That's when that little nagging thought crystalized. I realised this wasn't where I needed to be. I needed to be home. I needed to be North, needed to be doing more.

When I got to my apartment, I called my landlord, told him I was going to be gone at the end of the month. I called my girlfriend and told her the same thing. Asked her to come with me. My family thought she was great and she would be welcomed by them. She asked 'bout the rest of town and I didn't lie. Told 'er it wouldn't always be fun or easy but we would have each other. I told her my big plans to come home and open the first ever Pride Society in the Peace Country. I was so excited to have her with me on this but she told me that it would be too lonely.

I wish I could have stayed in Vancouver. But as I stood there at that crosswalk all those years ago. I saw those pride flags in the store windows, I realized I had never seen that up North. I couldn't stand the thought of another kid having to go through the same thing. So I moved back.

> *MELISSA is left staring at the world around her when the past begins to come crashing onto the stage.*

SCENE 4: BIKING AROUND

We are taken through time to childhood. Sounds of spring in a small town spill over the audience. Birds, trucks, dogs barking. It's a world that is both industrial and natural. The kids ride out on bikes. MELISSA watches them as they arrive, sinking into this memory. A pack of kids with lots of time on their hands.

ALICIA: Come on, keep up!

GREG: Hold on!

JULIA: Ugh, why are you riding on the sidewalk?

MELISSA: Why are you riding on the road?!?

JULIA: Because there is all this room!

> *JULIA zigzags all over the road.*

CANDICE: Car!

> *They all lean to one side except MELISSA who is on the sidewalk.*

GREG: Where are we going, by the way?

ALICIA: I dunno. Around.

CANDICE: Just around?

ALICIA: Yah.

CANDICE: Booooring!

JULIA: I want a cookie!

ALICIA: We could go get some from Muffin Break.

CANDICE: Yah!

GREG: No we can't go to Muffin Break! That's uptown. I can't go uptown.

ALICIA: Not even with your babysitter?

GREG: To get uptown we'd have to cross the highway, and I'm not allowed to cross the highway. So if my dad finds out I'll get a lickin'!

JULIA: Your dad never gives you a lickin'.

GREG: Wanna bet!

ALICIA: Hey! We can take the gully to get uptown.

MELISSA: I'm not allowed to go through the gully!

CANDICE: What!?! Who's not allowed to go in the gully?

MELISSA: Me!

CANDICE: WHY!?! It's the gully!

MELISSA: My mom says that there are bears and teenagers having sex in there!

> *They all laugh except for* MELISSA.

CANDICE: What does your mom know!

JULIA: Yah! Your family's new here! Your mom thinks there's bears everywhere!

GREG: Yah, new kid.

MELISSA: Don't call me that.

GREG: If your mom doesn't want you to go anywhere there are bears, you reeeallly shouldn't even be going to school.

JULIA: Right!

CANDICE: Yah tell your mom that you can't go anymore because of all the bears.

MELISSA: What are you talking about?

ALICIA: Last year a bear wandered onto the playground during school hours.

MELISSA: Onto the playground?!?

GREG: Yah! It went through all the garbages and then climbed the big yellow slide and just sat there.

CANDICE: They wouldn't let us go outside on lunch break until the rangers came and shot it!

JULIA: YAH! They shot it with a big gun. Blam!

JULIA lets go of the bike handlebars and rides with no hands.

MELISSA: They killed it?

ALICIA: They didn't kill it.

GREG: They just put it to sleep and then dragged it into a cage and drove off. Rangers have the best job! I wanna be one when I'm older.

CANDICE: As if! You're gunna run Dragon Palace when you grow up.

JULIA: Yah! Your dad's for sure gunna give you the restaurant.

ALICIA: Yur dad always says that you were born with a spatula in your hand.

GREG: He wishes.

MELISSA: Wait! So the bear's not dead.

ALICIA: Nope.

JULIA: It could have wandered back!

CANDICE: Yah, it could be in the gully!

GREG: Let's go find it!

MELISSA: No! My bike isn't for off-roading! What if it chases us?!

JULIA: Well you know what they say, "You don't have to outrun the bear—"

GREG, JULIA, & CANDICE: "—you just have to outrun the slowest person!"

MELISSA: Hey!

ALICIA: Cut it out. You're gunna make it so that she never comes on a bike ride with us again.

CANDICE: Spoilsport!

ALICIA: Listen up everyone. We're gunna take the gully.

MELISSA: Are you sure we have to?

ALICIA: Yes, it's the only way to get to Muffin Break without actually crossing the highway. We'll take the path behind Tucker Corner and go under the bridge. Loop back around near the airport and come up from the woods behind Muffin Break.

GREG: Yes!

JULIA: But you knooow, that means we will be riding in the gully for almost twenty minutes.

> *MELISSA slows her pedalling down.*

And you don't know the gully like we do. It would be easy for you to get lost. So let's go.

MELISSA: No!

CANDICE: Jules!

JULIA: What?!? I'm kidding, new kid. Learn to chill. Gosh.

ALICIA: Don't worry, I'll ride in the back to make sure we don't leave you behind. I don't think I'd get paid if I lost one of you to a bear.

CANDICE: Plus, the Gerards are always walking the trails now that they're retired. We can bike way faster than those old fogies can walk.

ALICIA: See. We'll be fine, new kid.

MELISSA: Don't call me new kid.

GREG: Well it's what you are.

CANDICE: Yah!

JULIA: It's just going to be that way till someone else moves here and has a kid in our grade.

MELISSA: Well how often does that happen?

CANDICE: Greg, when did Donald move here?

GREG: Kindergarten! In Mrs. C's class.

MELISSA: Who came after that?

JULIA: You did.

MELISSA: Four years!!! I might be the new kid for four years!?!?!

CANDICE: Maybe more.

GREG: Could be ten!

They all laugh. JULIA rides up to MELISSA.

JULIA: And even then, you'll still be a new kid compared to us.

ALICIA: Enough Julia. Come on, let's take the gully entrance behind the church.

They all lean in the same direction. They leave one by one, taking their bikes. Time speeds up and fast forwards us to the present. JULIA is now all grown up and has changed into workout gear.

SCENE 5: HELLO TO YOU TOO

JULIA has been riding for a while. She attacks the pedals. This is all part of her meditation. We hear a spin class instructor.

INSTRUCTOR: Riders this is it, we are climbing our last hill! Stand up out of the saddle. Your right foot is on the beat. Let's go! Right. Left. Right. Left. Hold that beat. Way to go riders. You got it. Reach down and add more tension. Drive it up! Up! UP! UP!

JULIA's cellphone rings.

JULIA: Hello?

ALICIA: Why are you panting?

JULIA: Spin class.

ALICIA: Oh.

JULIA: What do you want?

ALICIA: Mom's care home bill just came in the mail.

JULIA: Finally.

ALICIA: I told you that we needed to start paying as soon as she went into the home.

JULIA: Pay what? We needed to know how much her pension would cover before we knew how much we'd have to pay each month.

ALICIA: Whatever. It says we're two months behind now and that they're charging interest on what we owe. I'm on my way to the bank now to take care of it.

JULIA: Thanks.

ALICIA: I'll also set up auto-pay from my bank so make sure your half is there on time each month.

JULIA: It will be.

ALICIA: Okay.

JULIA: Okay.

ALICIA: I gotta go. I gotta run the girls to hockey.

JULIA: Wait.

ALICIA: What?

JULIA: I'll be heading up that way in a couple weeks.

ALICIA: Oh.

JULIA: Yeah.

ALICIA: Didn' think you'd have the time to come up so soon after the election.

JULIA: Neither did I but the House doesn't sit during spring break.

ALICIA: Well lemme know what day your flight arrives. I'll try to drive over to Fort St. John to pick you up.

JULIA: No need.

ALICIA: Who's picking you up?

JULIA: I'm gunna drive.

ALICIA: From John?

JULIA: No, the whole way up.

ALICIA: Oh.

JULIA: Yeah. I have a bunch of meetings with rural town councils along Highway 97.

ALICIA: That's a lot of driving.

JULIA: It is, but I think I might take some extra days off once I'm up there.

ALICIA: That'd be nice. It's been a while.

JULIA: You know, it's hard to get away.

ALICIA: Well, be careful near Hundred Mile House, there's a fire just northeast ah' town there. And another towards Burns Lake if you're heading that way.

JULIA: Thanks for the warning.

ALICIA: Make sure to give me the dates you're gunna be here so we can have the spare room ready for you.

JULIA: About that. They booked me a hotel room in town.

ALICIA: That's dumb. You know you can stay with us. The girls could use a sleepover with their aunty.

JULIA: I know. I'll come to the house for a visit.

ALICIA: Sure. Anyways, we can talk about this later, drive safe.

JULIA: Will do.

ALICIA: Okay. Gotta go. Bye.

JULIA hangs up.

JULIA sits on the bike for a bit, scrolling through her phone. She wipes herself down and takes her bike off stage. The lights of the studio spin class begin to flicker and morph.

SCENE 6: PROLIFERATION

The fire has grown. It is now beyond its infancy, but has yet to become full grown, as tall as trees. It slithers its way in the dry underbrush of the forest, consuming fallen trees, grass, and shrubs alike. It feeds on the ready-made kindling that is the underbrush. It whips bush to bush, furiously devouring these tender morsels of fuel. From here the fire has all it needs to grow into the monster that it can be.

SCENE 7: HOMECOMING

As the fire grows in the distance, we are welcomed into Muffin Break again. It is a hot, spring day months away from last fall's election.

JULIA: Hello?

CANDICE: *(off stage)* Be right there!

JULIA says nothing.

(as she enters) So what can I get— Fuck me!

JULIA: Hi . . .

CANDICE: Fuck me!

JULIA: . . .

CANDICE: Hoooooly shiiiit, fuuuuck meeee . . .

JULIA: Hi.

CANDICE: When did you roll in?

JULIA: Just now.

CANDICE: You fly up?

JULIA: No, I drove.

CANDICE: From Fort St. John?

JULIA: No, the whole way.

CANDICE: How long that take you?

JULIA: It should have been around twelve hours, if I did it in one go.

CANDICE: Oh, so when did you hit the road?

JULIA: Been driving for a little over a week now.

CANDICE: Gross, how come?

JULIA: They have me working over all the small-town mayors in this province.

CANDICE: That sucks.

JULIA: It's not too bad. It's an important job and it gets me some good face time with people.

CANDICE: Sure, sure.

JULIA: It's just a lot of driving though.

CANDICE: Didn't we once drive eighteen hours straight to Calgary for the Warped Tour?

JULIA: We were teens. Without lower back issues.

CANDICE: We are not that old! How do you have lower back issues?

JULIA: I dunno? But I do know I have to sleep with a knee pillow now.

CANDICE goes to the window.

CANDICE: Jeeeezuuuzzz . . . so that's what the salary of an MLA will get ya, hey?

JULIA: It's a rental.

CANDICE: Wow! Can't afford a house or a car living down south, hey.

JULIA: I have a home.

CANDICE: Oh sure sure. Size of a shoebox, I bet. Still don't own yourself a car though.

JULIA: I choose to not have a car.

CANDICE: I guess we are better off up 'ere, hey.

JULIA: It's very easy to get where I need by bus or bike!

CANDICE: Oh yah, yah. What's the charge time on one of those things?

JULIA: At a charging station, under an hour.

CANDICE: Otherwise?

JULIA: It can be a while. A couple days.

CANDICE: Holy shit! Days!?

JULIA: Only if you're charging on a regular wall plug at home. Besides, charge time didn't matter, it was one of our platform items. Provincial-wide phasing out of traditional ICE vehicles for ones that are low- or zero-emissions.

CANDICE: Oh yah, the green shift. Climate wise! Decarbonize! Economize!

JULIA: I see our campaign slogan sunk in.

CANDICE: Well ya'll were making a big deal about shouting it down there.

JULIA: It's a big deal everywhere.

CANDICE: You think so?

JULIA: We swept most of the province.

CANDICE: The Lower Mainland is not most of tha province.

JULIA: Hey we also made inroads into the Interior and the Island.

CANDICE: Yah yah.

JULIA: Won us the majority.

CANDICE: True.

JULIA: Now we just need to get the rest of the province on board.

CANDICE: Well hey, it's working, I started composting.

JULIA: That's a start . . .

CANDICE: And when folks come in, I tell 'em to start doing it as well. We all gotta do our part. Don't be part of the problem, be the solution.

JULIA: Sure, every little bit helps.

CANDICE: And ya know if I gotta rip up town for somethin', I make sure to not take the dually, it's diesel. Save on those carbon emissions.

JULIA: Well gas is also not good.

CANDICE: But sometimes in the summer I just gotta sit in the truck and crank that AC, it's way hotter up here than it used to be. Climate change, am I right bud?

JULIA: Well Candice, we need to stop thinking that it's the individual consumer's habits that's going to fix climate change. By tackling big industry—

JULIA cuts herself off and looks at CANDICE, who barrels over laughing.

CANDICE: You're too fucking easy!

JULIA: Fuck right off!

CANDICE: Oh careful you're an MLA now, don't wanna upset the constituents?

JULIA: Yur not from my fuckin' riding.

CANDICE: Ugh, that hurts. People will talk about this abuse.

JULIA: What people?

JULIA gestures to the empty store.

CANDICE: Oh I dunno, I mean, I've become a real pillar of the community up here. Folks actually listen to me now. I got pull!

JULIA: Har har.

CANDICE: What, s'not like the old days. I'm not getting tossed in the back of cop cars with your sorry ass anymore. I got the mayor on speed-dial now. I even had a write-up about this place a couple months ago in the *Alaska Highway News.*

JULIA: Wow, that's the big leagues.

CANDICE: Although that was about me shutting down.

JULIA: You're shutting down the Muffin Break!?

CANDICE: Sure as shit am.

JULIA: But it's an institution.

CANDICE: Institution or not, the writing is on the wall.

JULIA: There's gotta be something you can do?

CANDICE: Nothing's gunna save this place. The Muffin Break is like the Titanic. It's going down. Except unlike the Titanic, this captain's not going down with the ship.

JULIA: I mean maybe you could—

CANDICE: Nah. Once Timmies came to town it was only a matter of time.

JULIA: Yeah, I saw it as I drove in.

CANDICE: Super busy, right?

JULIA: I wouldn't say super busy . . .

CANDICE: I would! Look at that line of cars in the drive-through. Idiots flock to Timmies like it's their fucking patriotic duty or somethin'. Fucking sheep all of them.

JULIA: I don't get it.

CANDICE: Greg told me that they were looking for someone to franchise round here. But I thought it was better to keep the Muffin Break name going.

JULIA: Par for the course when it comes to Tims. They come to small towns and soon mom-n-pop shops close up.

CANDICE: I guess.

JULIA: Would you really have wanted to run a Tim Hortons?

CANDICE: Nah, I fuckin' hate those uniforms. Polyester pants give me the worst wedgies. And their menu fucking sucks. That's the best thing about this place, as long as I sell muffins I can sell whatever the fuck else I want.

    Beat.

I used to get the spillover when they were backed up with all the pipeline crews at shift change, at least. Tims couldn't handle the volume and I couldn't be more happy to have customers, even if I was their second choice.

JULIA: Candice, I didn't think cancelling the pipeline would drive you out of business.

CANDICE: Of course you didn't.

JULIA: We had to shut it down.

CANDICE: I know.

JULIA: It was a main item on our platform.

CANDICE: I know.

JULIA: We're trying to prove that we are willing to make the tough choice for the planet. The right choices.

CANDICE: I know all that all right. Jeezuz. Just 'cause it was the right thing to do, don't make it sting any less.

JULIA: I'm sorry.

CANDICE: Yah yah yah, enough of that. Let me get you a coffee while I still can. You still take it mostly milk, dash of actual coffee, and sweet like syrup?

JULIA: Uh if you could make it a double-shot caramel macchiato with oat milk, extra hot.

CANDICE gives her a look. JULIA laughs.

Black please.

CANDICE: You got it.

The world of Muffin Break begins to light up with all sorts of colours. The sky has made its way into the shop. It washes everything in their swirling cosmic colours. JULIA has made her way off stage leaving CANDICE alone, bathed in the lights.

The northern lights twinkle over us, timeless. They fill the space with magic as they dance through the sky. CANDICE stands witnessing them as they witness her.

CANDICE: I've lived in this area my whole life. I've never once thought I wanna be somewhere else. I never had the urge to pack it up and try my fortunes elsewhere. That thought never crossed my mind. And it's not like I haven't gone anywhere. I have done my fair share of travelling but I have yet to find a place that beats this valley. This valley is my home, why would I ever move away? Every life lesson I ever learned, I learned here. This place has always been home for my family. Literally.

When I was little, I would follow my dad around learning everything I could from him. Asking a million questions, never leaving a moment's silence for him to answer. Not that Dad cared, he didn't need to talk much. He liked to show more than tell. The only time he really flapped his gums was when he talked horses. People would come from all over the Peace to the reserve to meet him, because Dad was known for his talent with horses. And when I was old enough, he would let me help. But I never really got the hang of it. Didn't have the knack that my dad did. Didn't bother him though. He always said everyone had their talents and some folks just take time to find them.

Once I graduated high school I decided to move into town, told Mom and Dad that I needed to be more independent. They just laughed and said they didn't know if that was possible. Truth be told it was because I had no clue what to do with myself once my friends had all fucked off to college. Plus it was easier to get to work that way. I had just started working at the Muffin Break and morning shifts started real early in the only coffee shop in town. After years of working here, when old Mrs. Leffler asked if I wanted to buy the Muffin Break offa her, I jumped at the chance. I had witnessed just how much happened in a place like this. Breakups, first dates, birthdays, and wakes. Hushed conversions of where this week's bush party would be. Fist fights in the parking lot which I would then get in between when enough was enough.

This one time in fifth grade, I beat the shit out of a seventh grader for picking on me and my friends. The principal thought it best if I spent the rest of the day at home, to cool off. When I saw my dad coming to get me, through the office window, my boots started quaking. He poked his head in. Smiled at the receptionist, and then gave me a head nod to follow and walked out. I slipped quickly behind him and heard the principal tryin' tah get my dad to come back in for a chat.

"I got it, Mr. Bradshaw. I know how to talk to my daughter," he said.

Instead of going home we went and got lunch at Dixie Lee. We ate in silence until he asked, "Did you start it?" I shook my head. "I was just standin' up fur myself."

"Okay," he said.

"Dad, are you sure yur not mad at me?"

"I'm sure. You didn't start it, you were standin' up for somethin' when standin' up was needed. I taught you that."

So here I am in town. For better or for worse. And it used to be better, used to be a real bustling town, for how small it is. But now it's definitely for the worse. We lost ten percent of the jobs here when Canfor up and left. Nothing but a "we're sorry but we're just trying to create a 'more sustainable operating footprint.'" Families were left without any way to pay their bills. What do you expect them to do but move? We're haemorrhaging folks outta here now. People who have been this town's soul. People who like me have never had any other home but this valley.

I stand here, nose pressed up on the windows, watching families clear out in droves as one thing or another boards up behind them. And my brain makes sense of why they're leaving. Ya gotta do what it takes to survive. But my heart is screaming at them, why won't you fight for your home?

> *The northern lights begin to fade away as another moment of the past comes crashing onto the stage along with the former versions of CANDICE's friends.*

SCENE 9: WHERE ELSE DO WE GO

We are in front of the Muffin Break. CANDICE allows herself to be pulled into a time that once was. There is music playing. It's supposed to be a deterrent to loitering but with nowhere else to go in town it really isn't. We hear cars pull up and the opening of car doors. Lights go across the facade. A big truck pulls up and we can hear teens laughing. JULIA, MELISSA, and ALICIA enter. CANDICE watches them. She knows them so well.

MELISSA: I just don't understand why you didn't want to be roommates. We're both going to school in Vancouver, it would be so fun.

ALICIA: No trust me, you don't wanna room with a friend. It never goes well.

JULIA: Just 'cause yur unbearable and scared away all the friends you lived with, doesn't mean we couldn't live together.

MELISSA: Then why don't you wanna room together?

CANDICE: Because she's never actually liked you.

MELISSA: Fuck you, Candice!

MELISSA tries to give CANDICE a kick.

CANDICE: Ohh too slow.

JULIA: Missy, we're going to schools across town from each other. I don' wanna have tah get up at six just to get my ass to a 9 a.m. class. I barely make it to class on time now and I live a ten-minute walk away.

CANDICE: You still drive every day though.

JULIA: Well yah, I'm not a fuckin' loser.

MELISSA: But, Jules, it just seems silly that we wouldn't room together.

JULIA: Look. I know you're scared of having to make friends again, of being the new kid again. But we're all gunna be new kids at university.

MELISSA: But we don't have to do it alone, it'd be like having another sister to live with.

JULIA: Exactly! I can't stand my sister!

ALICIA: Fuck you too then. I can leave all y'all here if you hate me so much.

JULIA: You know what I mean, Al. We're always at each other's throats.

ALICIA: That is true.

JULIA: Missy, if we live together there is a big chance that we might end up getting fed up with each other's shit. We'll fucking start to leave little notes around the house like, like, "Don't touch my milk," "Sinks are for washing dishes, not storing them," or "Next time you borrow my top without asking I'll break your fuckin' arms!"

ALICIA: Fuckin' mean it too.

JULIA: It was one time!

MELISSA: Jules.

JULIA: Sorry. All *that* is to say that then one of us will move out in a huff. We'd never talk again.

MELISSA: I would hate that.

JULIA: Right? And ya know, I hear living in the dorms is an experience. Lots of new experimenting going on.

MELISSA: Okay. That sounds interesting.

JULIA: And if it really sucks we can get a place together in second year. Okay?

MELISSA: Deal.

They cheers beers.

CANDICE: That's if you survive till second year!

MELISSA: Shut up!

MELISSA chases CANDICE. GREG enters.

GREG: HEY MOTHER FUCKERS! PARTY TIME!

He has a 2-litre of Growers Cider.

ALICIA: Jeezus I dunno how ya drink that shit anymore. I mean it was fine for when you were fourteen but now. Yuck.

GREG: You coulda bought me something else when I asked for it.

ALICIA: And miss the chance to see you puke your guts out in front of the bonfire at Long Road. Never. Consider me your wise older sister, instigator of chaos.

JULIA: More like my sister Al, she is chaos.

ALICIA gives JULIA a good punch on the shoulder.

Owwww! Fuck you!

The sisters begin to wrastle. It doesn't last long as ALICIA clearly outclasses JULIA.

GREG: I want a muffin!

CANDICE: Greg, are you drunk already?

GREG: It's the Asian glow! Don't I look radiant?

MELISSA: I can't believe your dad has you booked for kitchen duty all summer long.

JULIA: Yah that sucks.

CANDICE: We were supposed to party all summer!

GREG: Nope. "You want to go to university, I'll pay for it. But you have to work in my kitchen. You're not here for party time." He only let me out tonight 'cause Al's driving.

ALICIA: That does sound like your dad!

CANDICE: It fuckin' sucks that you couldn't grad with us, G.

MELISSA: Yah!

GREG: Well, my folks were pretty freaked after they got a call from the hospital, telling them to come pick up their sixteen-year-old who just got his stomach pumped.

ALICIA: Oh that's nothing, kids are getting their stomachs pumped all the time here.

CANDICE: You sure it wasn't the stitches on your face?

GREG: Well there was that too.

    JULIA is in a headlock.

JULIA: Yah but still fuckin' sucks.

ALICIA: You ever figure out why they jumped you?

GREG: They didn't jump me.

CANDICE: Come on.

GREG: What? We were drunk and it all went a little too far. I threw the first punch.

CANDICE: That's not how it went down at all!

GREG: What do you know?

CANDICE: I know you were acting real jealous.

GREG: Gross, don't flatter yourself. You're like my sister.

CANDICE: Keep telling yourself that.

GREG: Look, I'm glad you didn't hook up with Lincoln, guy's a fuckin' asshole, but I didn't do anything about it.

CANDICE: Yah right!

GREG: Swear to fuckin' god!

CANDICE: All right, if you say so.

GREG: Can you imagine what people woulda said behind your back if you did though.

CANDICE: I can handle people talking shit about me.

GREG: Right, like how you handle your liquor?

CANDICE: Fuck you! I can drink with the best of 'em.

GREG: I bet you're a real fucking pro.

CANDICE: Oh go fuck yourself!

ALICIA: Do I have to sit on the two of you?

JULIA: She'll do it! Her ass is wide enough to cover two people!

> *ALICIA tickles JULIA.*

Fuck off! Stop! You know I hate this!

ALICIA: Exactly!

> *ALICIA tickles her for a bit then gets off of JULIA.*

JULIA: You suck!

ALICIA: Why thank you.

MELISSA: Wait, Lincoln was tryin' to hook up with you?

CANDICE: I was the one tryin' actually. He was just happy that I was even batting my eyes at him.

MELISSA: Then why'd you get jumped, G?

GREG: I didn't get jumped. Getting jumped means that they were lying in wait to beat me up. They just ganged up on me once it all started. But if I wasn't so drunk none of it woulda gone as far as it did.

CANDICE: Greg, you don't have to make excuses for them.

GREG: I'm not. It's the truth. When you went to take a piss, Linc started beakin' at me and I dunno how many jokes 'bout what kinda meat we serve at the restaurant I've heard assholes like him make. But when that same joke came out of his mouth I was just done and the alcohol wasn't helpin'. So I punched him. Then kept punchin' 'im, or tried to as the rest of them jumped on me. Then I was at the hospital. My mom was bawling her eyes out and my dad was yelling at me for being stupid and getting myself into that situation.

MELISSA: Fuck Candice, why didn't you tell us?!

CANDICE: Tell you what!?! That when I came out of the washroom, five guys were wailing on one of my best friends. Or that for the first time in my life I froze instead of throwin' down.

JULIA: Candice, I understand why you didn't jump into that mess, but I can't believe you didn't trust us enough to say you were there.

GREG: So what if she was. She's not the reason why I punched him. I chose to do something and I got what I got. I don't regret getting my ass kicked so badly. And I don't blame you for any of it, Candice. Understand?

CANDICE: Yah.

GREG: Don't get me wrong, I wasn't happy about not being here with you all this year but boy was it ever nice to be somewhere where I wasn't the only Asian kid in school. It's just that it pisses me off that my parents sent me to private school. I didn't get to walk into school on Monday as if it was nothing. I didn't get to show everyone I can take a whoopin' and what of it. Leaving just made it seem like I was scared. Running away.

JULIA: No one thinks you were scared. For fuck's sakes ya broke three of his front teeth. Who knew you got hammers for fists. They only kicked your ass 'cause it was five on one.

GREG: I guess that happens when you don't have family in this town. At least you two have each other.

> *GREG points to JULIA and ALICIA.*

MELISSA: We're probs gunna see them tonight.

JULIA: Oh most definitely.

MELISSA: You cool with that?

GREG: Yah why wouldn't I be. That was last year. I've grown up since moving to the city. I've matured.

> *We hear the sound of a big truck doing a smoke show. Followed by the sound of a bunch of other trucks starting up and driving off with different sounds of music blasting from each of them.*

ALICIA: All right, dorks. Looks like folks are headed out to Long Road now. Let's get in the car and go!

CANDICE: Can we do a few loser laps 'round town so we're not standing around while they try an' light the pallets.

ALICIA: Fine by me. Those idiots just filled a jerry can and I would rather not burn off my eyebrows seeing as I just plucked today.

CANDICE: Let's do this!

MELISSA: Shotgun!

JULIA: Fuck you! That seat has my name on it.

> *They all run off except for CANDICE. A truck backs up and then goes forward. Headlights go over the front of Muffin Break. The roar of cars fills our ears and then dies away.*

SCENE 10: HOLY SHIT

We arrive back in the present. CANDICE is standing behind the counter of Muffin Break. She stands there still holding onto the memory that has just floated through. JULIA enters from outside, snapping CANDICE back to reality.

JULIA: Hey thanks for letting me plug in my car.

CANDICE: No problem. Sorry we don't have any charging stations in town yet.

JULIA: It's fine, didn't think there'd be one.

CANDICE: I'll send the cost of the juice to your riding office once I get the hydro bill back.

JULIA: Well I have cash I can give you now.

CANDICE: It was a joke.

JULIA: Right, I get jokes.

CANDICE: So did you have any troubles findin' a charge on your way up?

JULIA: Surprisingly no. Only real worry was between here 'n Prince.

CANDICE: Oh?

JULIA: Yeah, I thought there would be one at Mackenzie Junction but I had to roll into Mackenzie proper to find one.

CANDICE: Oh yah, makes sense. Get you fancy city slickers stopping for a charge then hope you spend some cash in town. Too bad there's not much tah do there.

JULIA: It was nice, the weather was surprisingly warm for this time of year so I walked around town.

CANDICE: Well get ready for a big fuckin' surprise. It's gunna be thirty-five degrees tomorrow.

JULIA: That's too warm for March.

CANDICE: No fuckin' duh, it's not helping that little forest fire we got going on out at Jackfish that's creeping towards town.

JULIA: What? Really?

CANDICE: Yah, they had to evac the area a few days ago but there's not many people out that way anymore so that helped.

JULIA: Shit.

CANDICE: I'm actually surprised you didn't say anything about all the smoke in town when you got here.

JULIA: Honestly it's been like this almost the whole way up so I guess I didn't think twice about there being smoke here.

CANDICE: Well the whole province is pretty used to having smoke-filled summers now, isn't it?

JULIA: You know the reason for that right.

CANDICE: Yah I'm not ignorant.

JULIA: I'm just saying.

CANDICE: Yur just sayin', yur just sayin'. You an' yur party are just sayin' a lot of things. None of it makes anyone up here feel like you give a fucking shit about them.

JULIA: But the party does.

CANDICE: Oh, I'm sure you think you do, bud.

JULIA: Look we needed to and still need to make drastic changes to our ways of living and that starts with how extractionist and colonial the gas and oil industry is.

CANDICE: Your gunna lecture me on colonialism?

JULIA: Of course not, I'm not that ignorant.

CANDICE: Ignorant or not, I still gotta see your sorry face on TV criticizing everything this town does to survive. We are not the villains here, Jules.

JULIA: I never said you were. Stop making it about heroes and villains. All of you need to realize that the good old days of industry-first are gunna come crashing down.

CANDICE: Don't fuckin' yell at me about it. I understand what needs to get done, Jules.

JULIA: Sorry. It's been a long drive up and all these meetings haven't really been warm receptions.

CANDICE: I can imagine. Should of seen the fucking looks of shock when I campaigned for your stupid party.

JULIA: Oh.

CANDICE: I had this place all done in your party's colours. Signs, pamphlets, the whole nine yards. Prob'ly what put the final nail in the Muffin Break coffin, more'n shutting down a lousy pipeline. But I couldn't not fight for you an' yur party.

JULIA: At least one person understands up here.

CANDICE: All your platform points make sense. They just don't make us feel good. You talk about how there are going to be sacrifices that need to be made. That scares the people up here. People you know and grew up with. Your fucking family, for fuck's sakes. Have you forgotten that we need fossil fuel so we don't freeze tah death in minus forty weather? Or that most folks can't afford an electric heat pump that fuckin' works when it's that cold outside. You're askin' everyone to believe in you an' take a leap of faith. But all we ever get is judgement for the way we have to survive up here. And that sure doesn't make us feel like leaping.

Ya don' think that we also see how fucked we are? Last year Tumbler had to fuckin' evacuate because of the forest fires. Half of them went tah Dawson, the other half made it this way. They were all living in the rec centre while Tumbler fuckin' burned tah the ground. Most folks never went back. Nothin' to go back to. Those that did are now waiting till something gets done about it. You got folks holed up in emergency housing, knees knocking, scared they're one of those sacrifices your party keeps talking about.

JULIA: I'm sorry.

CANDICE: For fuck sakes Julia, I'm not looking for an apology. I'm on your side. While you were marching on Victoria to stop Site C, I was paddling the Peace, boots on the ground, trying to make sure they couldn't start. Almost everyone in the area was there.

What I need ya to do is to not talk like we're all idiots up here who don't see that the world is on fire. We just have very little options without losing everything we value or letting our kids go hungry.

JULIA: I— Okay.

Beat.

CANDICE: So you plan on seeing anyone else while yur up?

JULIA: Well I'm going to have dinner with Alicia and her girls at some point but we haven't set anything yet.

CANDICE: You're not staying with them?

JULIA: No.

CANDICE: Why not? They have pleny'a space. An' it's twenty minutes outta town so you would hardly see anyone ya don't wanna.

JULIA: I need Wi-Fi for work.

CANDICE: Right.

JULIA: I booked a room at the hotel.

CANDICE: Not in one of our historic motels?

JULIA: Ha, no.

> *MELISSA enters and heads straight to the counter. She looks in the back to see how the coffee is doing while unpacking her thermos.*

MELISSA: Hey, Candice.

CANDICE: Hey, Mel, how's it going, bud?

MELISSA: Oh you know, can't complain. Coffee ready?

CANDICE: Just started a new pot, it'll be a few.

MELISSA: Right on. Hey, Julia, how ya doing? . . . Julia! Oh my god! Julia! You're here. Wow. Fuck. Wow. Umm. Have you been there the whole time? When did ya roll in? I mean how are you? Or uh, how have you been? It's been a while. How many years? Lots. Shit Wow. Okay, let me just—

MELISSA goes to leave.

CANDICE: Whoa there. Settle down champ.

MELISSA: Right. Shit! You must be mad.

JULIA: About?

MELISSA: Leaving my truck running. I was just zipping in I swear. I was just coming to fill my thermos on my way to work. I'm on afternoons this week and Muffin Break's coffee is better than the piss they serve in the break room.

CANDICE: For fuck's sakes, she'll be even more mad if you stand there flapping your gums without actually turning off your truck. Go!

MELISSA: Right. One sec.

MELISSA leaves. JULIA and CANDICE laugh.

JULIA: So that hasn't changed.

CANDICE: Her not being able to make a decision?

JULIA: No, you barkin' orders at her.

CANDICE: Oh yah, well otherwise we coulda been here another twenty minutes watchin' her doing doughnuts like a dog trying to bite its own ass.

MELISSA comes back.

MELISSA: Okay. There. Hi!

JULIA: Hi.

MELISSA: Oh my god! You're here! Wow. It's good to see you.

JULIA: Same.

MELISSA: When did you roll in?

JULIA: Today.

MELISSA: You fly up?

JULIA: No, I drove.

MELISSA: From John?

JULIA: No.

MELISSA: From Prince?

JULIA: The whole way up.

MELISSA: How long that take you?

JULIA: About a week and a half.

MELISSA: Holy shit! You should be able to make that drive in one go, right?

JULIA: Had meetings along the way.

MELISSA: Aw yah, aw yah.

CANDICE: It's only about twelve hours tops if you straight shot it.

MELISSA: I made it in ten and a half hours once. Only stopped to pee and gas up.

JULIA: Wow.

MELISSA: Well I just wanted to make it here as quick as I could.

JULIA: You also have a lead foot from what I remember.

MELISSA: What?!? No!

CANDICE: Bullshit! You do! How much was that ticket you got there last week?

MELISSA: $630.

JULIA: What?!?!? How fast were you going?

MELISSA: Only a buck forty.

CANDICE: Only 140?!?!

MELISSA: Yah and it was only $600 because I was going double the speed limit in a construction zone!

CANDICE: MELISSA!

MELISSA: What, no one was working!

> *JULIA laughs a deep belly laugh. Maybe it's been years since a sound like that has escaped from her lungs.*

Have you had lunch yet?

JULIA: Nope.

MELISSA: Wanna hit up Dragon Palace? It'd be great to catch up.

JULIA: Right now?

MELISSA: Yah, why not!

CANDICE: Aren't you on your way to work?

MELISSA: Right, fuck.

CANDICE: Besides, she hasn't even checked into her room yet.

MELISSA: You're staying in a motel?

JULIA: No, the new hotel.

MELISSA: Oooh.

CANDICE: She wants to try the water slide.

MELISSA: Oh me too!

JULIA: Nooo, I need a place that's quiet and private.

MELISSA: How about you crash at my place? I have Wi-Fi, plenty of space, and it wouldn't be a bother.

JULIA: No that's okay.

MELISSA: More'n welcome to.

JULIA: I have early morning meetings with my riding office every day before I hit the road to meet with local town councils.

MELISSA: You're up for a bit then?

JULIA: Yeah till Monday.

MELISSA: Great! Then we have pleny'a time for a few drinks before ya go then.

JULIA: Yeah for sure. And how about you? How have you been?

MELISSA: Oh you know, can't complain. Work keeps me busy.

JULIA: You still workin' at West Fraser?

MELISSA: Yup! Still at the mill. They can't get rid of me. Unless you know they shut down like Canfor did, then I guess I won't have a choice, will I?

JULIA: Yeah I guess not.

CANDICE: Stop bumming her out! Tell her about all the volunteering you do. You're so philanthropic.

MELISSA: Shut your dirty mouth, she doesn't need to hear about all that!

CANDICE: Fucking tell her!

JULIA: Yeah tell me!

MELISSA: Ugh, well if ya must know. I'm helping run the Pride Society outta Dawson Creek there.

JULIA: That's awesome! So then is that rainbow crosswalk over by the 7-Eleven your work?

MELISSA: It is. It's not much but we're trying to get them in all the towns round here. Along with scraping the cash together to expand across the region. You know, so kids don't have to drive all the way to Dawson for a place to gather.

JULIA: Cool. How are folks taking that?

MELISSA: You know, it's not as bad as I thought it'd be. But there's still some fucking pricks though. Doing fucking burnouts on the crosswalks or painting 'em black.

CANDICE: Fucking idiots.

MELISSA: Well, we'll keep paintin' 'em back. We aren't going anywhere, it's just tough to get people to change their ways right?

JULIA: Yeah you're telling me.

MELISSA: Ya shur about staying inna hotel?

JULIA: I'm sure.

MELISSA: 'Cause you know me, I sleep like a rock. 'Member when we had that sleepover in grade six? An' you woke up on the other side a' me in the mornin' because ya rolled right over me an' I didn't even notice?

JULIA: *(laughing)* Yeah.

MELISSA: Oh shit! I gotta go.

CANDICE: Did you want a coffee before you go?

MELISSA: No time! I'll buy two tomorrow!

CANDICE: And what if I'm not open tomorrow?

MELISSA: When you finally get around to boarding this place up, I'll get around to finding a new coffee place.

CANDICE: You're such a pain.

JULIA: Been one since the first day you moved here.

MELISSA: You both love it.

> *Smoke begins to fill the stage and time begins to slow down. A red deadly hue, the colour of live embers, of a raging hot heat, overtakes the stage.*

SCENE 11: ACCELERATION

The fire is alive now and will be for a long time. What keeps it alive are these intense hot embers. They pulse like breath and are able to grow unnoticed. It will consume all that has been drying out. It will feed continuously without humans to monitor it. Anything still alive and green will now wither from the heat of it. It breathes and grows and breathes and grows. Gaining speed and intensity over time till the treetops explode. Rushing over us.

SCENE 12: RIDING IN CARS

The sound of a car radio fires up. Searching for a signal. Bleeps of life filter through and then it begins to settle on a station. The stereo blasts the music loud. We are hurtling down the highway, years in the past, back to when they were teens.

MELISSA: Do you think we can head to the party now?

ALICIA: You fuckin' kiddin' me?

MELISSA: What?

JULIA: It's a fuckin' party, not class.

CANDICE: Yah, Missy, they probably haven't even lit the bonfire yet.

MELISSA: But but what if the cops bust it up quickly tonight?

ALICIA: Wha'? Nah. Well. Nah.

GREG: Padiddle!

ALICIA, JULIA, & CANDICE: PADIDDLE!!!

MELISSA: What?!? No!!

ALICIA, JULIA, CANDICE, & GREG: DRINK! DRINK! DRINK!

MELISSA: Fuck you guys!

They all laugh as MELISSA takes a large swig.

Ugh . . . I hate chugging

GREG: Then don't suck.

CANDICE: Yah be faster eh!

MELISSA: Fuck you! Give me a—

ALICIA, JULIA, CANDICE, & GREG: PADIDDLE!!!

MELISSA: Nooooooo!

ALICIA, JULIA, CANDICE, & GREG: DRINK! DRINK! DRINK!

MELISSA: Seriously.

> *They all laugh as* MELISSA *takes a large swig.*

I swear th—

ALICIA, JULIA, CANDICE, & GREG: PADIDDLE!!! DRINK! DRINK! DRINK!

MELISSA: Fuuucck!!!

> *They all laugh as* MELISSA *takes a large swig.*

Okay please no more!

JULIA: Can't quit, thems da rules bud.

ALICIA: As long as yur in this car.

MELISSA: Yah yah, then let me out. Imma puke.

ALICIA: You better not.

MELISSA: Just let me out!

ALICIA: Jeezuz, fucking gimme a sec ta pull over.

JULIA: You better hurry.

CANDICE: I think I can see it coming up!

GREG: Puke that way! Not on me!

ALICIA: There. Fucking hustle! Get out!

The car idles on the side of the road.

MELISSA: Move!

MELISSA pushes GREG out of the car and he lands on his ass. CANDICE and JULIA crack up. MELISSA gets out of the car. GREG goes to follow her but keeps going past her.

CANDICE: Gunna hold her fuckin' hair back, Greggy?

GREG: Fuck that! I gotta yes-yes in French!

GREG runs off stage looking for a place to pee.

JULIA: Go Greg! Whip it out! Give us a show!

CANDICE: Helicopter! HELICOPTER!

JULIA and CANDICE catcall and holler at GREG. MELISSA meanwhile has set up camp at the back bumper, hunched over, heaving. ALICIA looks in the rear-view mirror.

ALICIA: Hey! Lightweight, don't get any on the car!

JULIA sticks her head out the window to look.

JULIA: Ah fuck, it's all just foam. It's just fucking foam you fuckin' wuss! Suck it up! Puke and rally!

MELISSA: FUCK OFF!

> *JULIA and CANDICE laugh. CANDICE cracks a drink. She notices that it is about to foam over so she starts to drink it fast.*

CANDICE: Oh fuck, fuck, fuck!

ALICIA: Fuck off.

CANDICE: I got it, I got it!

JULIA: Go! Go! Go!

ALICIA: Idiots.

JULIA: Who's the idiot who said we could drink in 'ere?

ALICIA: Drink. Not spill and puke.

JULIA: Yur tha one that said, *(imitating ALICIA)* "As long as yur in this car, you either play padiddle or walk."

ALICIA: She's only had like two swigs.

JULIA: Three!

ALICIA: Three.

JULIA: Three big fuckin' swigs.

ALICIA: Whatever! She should be able to hold her liquor! For fuck's sakes!

MELISSA: *(from outside the car)* I can hold my liquor! It's just f—

> *MELISSA starts heaving. CANDICE and JULIA laugh.*

ALICIA: Is it getting on the car?

CANDICE: It's just foam.

ALICIA: I don't fuckin' care. It's my fucking car, I'll leave her here tah walk tah the party if I fuckin' want.

JULIA: Hooooly, fuckin' calm down.

CANDICE: Yah, not like it's brand new or anything. Jeez.

ALICIA: Why the fuck does that matter? It's my car and she could be a half-fucking decent person and take a couple steps away from the car as she pukes.

JULIA: Oh come on, Al.

ALICIA: You wanna fuckin' join 'er?

JULIA zips her lips. ALICIA looks out the side window.

GREG, coming back to the car, gets in, opens a beer, and is about to take a drink when he notices the awkward silence in the car along with the sound of MELISSA dry heaving.

GREG: Seems real pleasant in here. What'd I miss?

CANDICE: Al got real touchy about Missy puking on her car.

GREG: Who wouldn't be pissed if someone puked on their grad present.

JULIA and CANDICE look at ALICIA. MELISSA gets into the car, shoving GREG to the middle seat.

MELISSA: Would you rather I puked in here?

ALICIA: I woulda kicked your ass.

MELISSA: As if.

ALICIA: I can step outside right now if you like.

MELISSA: I'm good thanks.

JULIA: Yah just get us to the party already.

ALICIA: Please?

JULIA: Get us to the party please.

ALICIA puts the car in drive and they take off on the road again.

GREG: So Al, you think your gunna head back to college next year?

ALICIA: I don't think so.

GREG: Why not? Yur dad's outta the hospital.

ALICIA: I figure Mom could use the help with bills. Plus she's gunna be taking Dad to all kinds of specialists.

JULIA: He may be out of the hospital but he's far from a hundred percent.

ALICIA: And someone's gotta babysit Julia this summer while Mom's running Dad all over the province and working.

JULIA: Fuck you, I don't need a babysitter.

ALICIA: You sure about that? I seem to recall getting you outta the drunk tank last year while Mom was living in the hospital taking care of Dad.

GREG: Really?

CANDICE: Yah. Not her best moment.

ALICIA: Sure wasn't.

JULIA: Well don't let me be the one stopping you from going back.

ALICIA: You're not, but no one's gunna make me go back either. And truthfully, it's not really my thing.

GREG: Oh well, why waste the time right?

ALICIA: Right, Greg, my boy.

GREG: Oohhh so then does Jules get the car when she goes to college?

ALICIA: Yah fucking right, it's my car even if I moved back. This is one thing I don't have to share with her.

JULIA: No fucking duh, you tell me every time I ask to borrow it.

GREG: Hey, I'm sure your mom might surprise you at grad with your own car.

JULIA: Oh I'm sure I won't be getting one. Only Alicia gets big gifts like a car.

ALICIA: Listen, Mom is working her ass off to save up for your un-i-ver-sity, even though she sure as shit doesn't have the money to do so. Sorry she can't also throw in a car. You better get that bug out of your ass and be thankful you get to go at all. You're reeaal fucking lucky that Mom is as stubborn as a rock and refuses to ask you to help pay your tuition.

Silence.

MELISSA opens another drink.

MELISSA: For your information, Al. I can hold my liquor.

ALICIA: Sure seems like it.

MELISSA: I just can't fucking slam beers.

JULIA: Then why did you ask for beer?

MELISSA: I like beer—*to sip*, not drink as fast as it can go down my throat! Makes too much fizz.

ALICIA: Fine.

MELISSA: Nothing got on the car by the way.

JULIA: Told you.

ALICIA: It better of not.

MELISSA: Sorry that we made you mad, Al.

ALICIA: It's okay.

CANDICE, JULIA, & GREG: *(like children)* Yah, sorry Alicia!

ALICIA: Oh fuck off I'm not your babysitter anymore.

JULIA: Yah guys! She's our chauffeur and bootlegger!

ALICIA punches JULIA in the arm.

ALICIA: Punch buggy padiddle

JULIA: OWW!

CANDICE, MELISSA, & GREG: PADIDDLE! DRINK! DRINK! DRINK!

> *JULIA takes a big swig. The music comes back in. They recognize the song and turn it up. It's Mariah Carey's "Fantasy." They all begin to sing together. The kids car dance together. The lights shift, they leave except for JULIA and CANDICE who remain. We are ripped back to the present.*

Back at Muffin Break. It's later in the day. JULIA is seated, looking out the window.

CANDICE: You still with us?

JULIA: What?

CANDICE: Didn't think so. Work?

JULIA: No. Well not really. Actually just looking at this place.

CANDICE: This place?

JULIA: All of it. In here. Out there. Wondering what's gunna happen to you all.

CANDICE: Sure is an interesting time for you to be here.

JULIA: That's putting it mildly.

CANDICE: Yah well doesn't really help tah constantly be talkin' 'bout how they still haven't contained that fire out at Jackfish. Every morning when I come to open up that sun is just a bit more orange. Whole town's startin' tah get ready to take action if need be.

JULIA: That's what forest firefighters are for. Should probably worry more about getting out intact.

CANDICE: Should, but we won't. You know folks round here, Jules. They're gunna help however they can. But there's no need fur you tah worry 'bout that.

JULIA: Kinda hard not to when I look out these windows at those skies and fucking can't believe they're still mining coal out at Willow Creek. Like what are folks up here not getting?

CANDICE: Let's not go down that road again.

JULIA: Okay.

CANDICE: What I was tryin' tah say is that we're more'n just industry, ya know. This is our home.

JULIA: Not my home anymore.

CANDICE: Bullshit.

JULIA: I haven't lived here since high school.

CANDICE: This is still your home though.

JULIA: I don't recognize anyone anymore.

CANDICE: Oh that's nothing big, everyone's still here, just a bit more weathered than you remember. And most of the guys are balder too.

JULIA: Candice!

CANDICE: It's true though! You still have that image of what everyone looked like in high school. You got to hold onto that version of us. I've had to watch everyone else get uglier over time.

> *JULIA laughs.*

Can I get you anything else besides that cup of coffee you've been nursing all day?

JULIA: No I'm good, thanks.

CANDICE: How's your mum? She's in that old fogey's compound north of the Co-op there in Dawson, right?

JULIA: Yeah, Rotary Manor. She's doing all right. They take decent care of her there. She told us to kill her before we ever put her in a home but she is better off there.

CANDICE: That's good to hear.

JULIA: Yeah.

CANDICE: Must be weird seeing her in a home.

JULIA: I actually haven't been to visit yet.

CANDICE: Really?

JULIA: Really. Alicia took care of all the arrangements. Packed her up, moved her in. Never asked for help. Told me to focus on the election. I bet when I do get out to see Mum though it is going to be weird.

CANDICE: Shit.

JULIA: And like, she was—she is fierce. You know, she fucking called out Principal Bradshaw for being a racist?

CANDICE: Yah right!

JULIA: Seriously. You know how in grade seven, I got kicked off the class trip to Vancouver for copying homework?

CANDICE: I know yur mum came down and had words with the principal.

JULIA: It was mor'n just words. Turns out a couple of other kids had been caught cheating on a test but they were still going on the trip. When Mum found out, she fucking let the teacher have it. A few days later Principal Bradshaw calls Mum to say I'm allowed to rejoin the class trip. But Mum tells 'em, "No thank you, Julia does not need to be on a trip with racists like you," and just hung up the phone.

CANDICE: Oh shit! Wasn't Principal Bradshaw her boss?

JULIA: Yeah!

CANDICE: Fucking Stella!!!

JULIA: She's had to deal with so much garbage her whole life and took it all with a fuckin' smile. Even when she looked after Dad full-time until he died. And now she doesn't get to live out her life in her own home with those beautiful memories of their life together. She's losing them all and will just be void of everything that made her my mom. I'm so afraid that I'm not going to be able to stop crying if I go see her. And she won't know why and all she'll want to do is try to make me feel better and that will only make the tears fall harder.

CANDICE: Jules, I'm so sorry.

JULIA: It's fine. I'm gunna use the washroom.

JULIA leaves for the washroom. ALICIA walks in the door.

ALICIA: Hey, C.

CANDICE: Hey, Al.

CANDICE: How's things?

ALICIA: Fine. You?

CANDICE: Slammed like always.

ALICIA: Looks like it.

CANDICE: What can I do ya for?

ALICIA: Killing time before heading over to the girls' hockey practice.

CANDICE: Right! The girls' sandwiches. I'll go get those ready.

ALICIA: Oh no rush, thanks though.

CANDICE: Completely slipped my mind today, sorry.

ALICIA: No worries.

CANDICE: Been a little preoccupied.

ALICIA: Understandable. When's your last day?

CANDICE: Dunno fur sure. Soon.

ALICIA: Just makes me sad thinking about this place being all closed up.

CANDICE: Hey yur more'n welcome to try and go up against Timmies yourself.

ALICIA: Yah right, bud. I have enough stress running one business.

CANDICE: Fair enough.

JULIA comes back in.

JULIA: Hey.

ALICIA: Hey.

Beat.

Thought you'd still be on the road?

JULIA: I was, just rolled in.

ALICIA: Right. How was the drive from Prince?

JULIA: Uh, pretty good.

ALICIA: How was the Pass?

JULIA: Clear once I got up out of the smoke at the summit there. But man, the trees are like gone.

ALICIA: You betcha. That side of town got hit hard last year with fire. It was just waiting to go up too. Pine beetle left it all dead and the heat dried up the underbrush. So one idiot smoker was all it took.

CANDICE: Your sister and her girls had to crash with me when they got the evac order.

JULIA: Holy shit, why didn't you tell me?

ALICIA: It was fine. We just parked the holiday trailer in C's driveway for a couple days. Wasn't even that close really, nothing like this one.

JULIA: Yeah I don't remember it ever getting this smokey when we were kids.

CANDICE: That's for sure.

ALICIA: Mmhmm.

CANDICE: You two good? Need anything else?

JULIA: Nope.

ALICIA: All good.

CANDICE: Okay, I'll just be packing those sandwiches up in the back. Shout if you need anything.

CANDICE heads to the back.

ALICIA: Why are you hanging out here?

JULIA: I figured I'd say hi to Candice while I waited until I could check in to my hotel room.

ALICIA: I still don' get why you just don' stay with us? Saves you money.

JULIA: I don't need to save the money. I have a travel budget.

ALICIA: Yah whatever. Why didn't you stop at the house first?

JULIA: I wasn't sure if you'd be there. So I came here to see a friendly face.

ALICIA: How'd you know she'd be friendly? You two haven't really kept in touch.

JULIA: Took a chance. Besides, coming here was better than wandering around town for folks to stare at me trying to figure out just who this stranger is.

ALICIA: Whatever, it's your home. We all know who you are.

JULIA: It's my hometown, my home is down south.

ALICIA: That's just where you pay rent.

JULIA: I am doing more than just paying rent. I'm not sure if you remember, but I was just voted into office, I've got responsibilities.

ALICIA: Yah I know but in four years who's to say you'll still have that job.

JULIA: Who's to say that in five years you'll have one.

ALICIA: All I'm saying is that you seem to forget that you can always come back here for good if ya want.

JULIA: God, I hope not.

ALICIA: What's wrong with living here?

JULIA: Nothing. It's just . . .

ALICIA: What?

JULIA: I don't think I could live here anymore.

ALICIA: Oh come on, Jules.

JULIA: It's true.

ALICIA: Bull fuckin' shit. You were born here, grew up here, this will always be your home.

JULIA: Okay.

ALICIA: Anyways. When'd ya wanna come by the house for supper?

JULIA: Whenever it works for you, also if you have the time I'd like to treat you all for once.

ALICIA: So you did decide to spend some time up here.

JULIA: I'm only here till Monday. I have four town councils in the area to meet with before hitting the road back. That's why I got a room here in town, so I could stay in one place for a couple of nights and have the weekend to hang out.

ALICIA: Oh, that will be nice. I guess you could also stop in and see Mom when yur in Dawson.

JULIA: Yeah, that's the plan.

ALICIA: She'll like that.

JULIA: That's if my meeting doesn't go past visiting hours.

ALICIA: Whatever, just go by and see her. They'll let you sneak in if you tell them you're Stella's little girl. They love her there and she can't stop telling them 'bout Julia who's really made something of herself in the big city.

JULIA: Alicia, you've done amazing for yourself.

ALICIA: Oh I don't give a shit. She's not doing it on purpose, just where she's at mentally.

JULIA: Will she even know I'm there.

ALICIA: She might, she might not. Depends on where she's at that day. You could always call ahead and ask the nurses how she is.

JULIA: That sounds good. I'll do that.

ALICIA: Either way you should go. You haven't seen her for a while. You can spare a half-hour to sit with her.

JULIA: I know.

ALICIA: And you weren't around to help me get her into the home.

JULIA: I know.

ALICIA: It's not like yur gunna be any less busy now that yur in office.

JULIA: I know.

ALICIA: Just go see her.

JULIA: Okay. Does she remember that we sold her house?

ALICIA: No, she still thinks she's gunna walk out of there and go back to living solo.

JULIA: She loved that house. I'm sure she just wants to be home.

ALICIA: Of course she does. That's all she ever talks about. But you and I know, Mom needs to be under constant care. I can't do that for her, and you certainly can't. We both agreed that it was time to move her and to sell the house so that we could set aside that cash for her care.

JULIA: I know but—

ALICIA: Fuck, Jules, I wish I could have been like Mom and dropped everything to take care of her like she did with Dad. But few people have that kind of strength. I've got my own business to run and two young girls to raise and you have tah run the fucking government.

JULIA: I don't run the government.

ALICIA: You know what I mean. If you had been here at all in the last decade you would have seen how bad it got. The struggle it was to get her to agree to move. The heartbreak in her eyes every time I had to remind her why all her things were in boxes and that no, Dad wasn't just at work. You weren't here for any of that.

JULIA: That's not fair Alicia, you don't understand my level of commitments. The time and effort activism takes. To be on the front lines of change. How much I had to hustle to even get this far.

ALICIA: What I understand is that all your stuff comes first, everything else second.

JULIA: I'm sorry I couldn't do more.

ALICIA: You could have but you didn't.

JULIA is speechless.

ALICIA: Go see her or don't. It's up to you.

JULIA: I will. I'll go see her.

ALICIA: All right, I gotta go. The girls are almost done hockey practice. I'll call you later.

JULIA: Sounds good.

ALICIA: *(to CANDICE)* Hey you have those sandos ready to go for the team?

CANDICE: *(coming out from the back)* Sure do. Also threw in some juice boxes and orange slices.

ALICIA: You're the best!

CANDICE: It's all parta being the team sponsor.

ALICIA: Well it won't be the same now that you're closing up.

CANDICE: Maybe Timmies will give you their day-old Timbits.

ALICIA: Mmm, rock-hard doughnut holes.

They laugh.

I'll pull round back and load up.

CANDICE: Sure thing, just let yourself in, it's open.

ALICIA: Got it. I'll text you later, Jules.

ALICIA leaves.

JULIA: See ya.

CANDICE: Man, that sister of yours never slows down.

JULIA: Nope. She's just like my mom.

CANDICE: You okay?

JULIA: Yeah. Team sponsor?

CANDICE: Oh yah! Been the sponsor for years. The Muffin Break Broncos.

JULIA: Wow.

CANDICE: It's mostly just offsetting some of the costs so that all the kids can get new jerseys and gear when they need it. Make sure no one drops out 'cause they can't afford the equipment.

JULIA: That's so awesome.

CANDICE: I'll keep doing what I can next year but with one of the mills closed up who knows if we'll be able to have a team.

JULIA: Wish we had a team sponsor when we were kids. Maybe I could have played a few more years after Dad got sick. Instead of trading in my hockey stick for a name tag at Peoples Drug Mart.

CANDICE: No shit, we coulda used ya. You were fucking vicious.

JULIA: I was not.

CANDICE: Fuck that, you totally were. Every time you laid someone out, they took a few extra seconds to get back up.

JULIA: Mmm, that was so much fun.

CANDICE: See! Ya fuckin' goon!

They laugh.

JULIA: Okay I should go check in. Thanks for the coffee.

CANDICE: No prob.

JULIA goes to leave.

Hey Julia, I'm glad you're in town.

JULIA: That's nice to hear.

CANDICE: Why don't you come back after you settle in. We can have some drinks here once I'm all closed up. Order some food.

JULIA: I have to get up pretty early.

CANDICE: It would be nice to have the company.

JULIA: Sure.

> *The Muffin Break is suddenly filled with an orange glow as CANDICE and JULIA walk off stage. In shadow ALICIA steps out, gazing at the sky.*

SCENE 14: ALICIA

ALICIA stands on the stage as the orange lights fill the stage. Smoke begins to creep into view. It is eerie. The northern lights are not the colour they should be. Nothing is.

ALICIA: Life isn't fair.

That's what my dad said as we boarded the plane from Guatemala to Canada. "Life isn't fair, so there's no use crying about it, Alicia." He then knelt down and wiped my tear-soaked cheeks and said, "But that doesn't mean it's wrong to cry," as streams of water poured down his own face.

We cry a lot in our family. I remember Abuela shed tears every day when we finally visited. Instead of being overjoyed and showering us with hugs and kisses, she was holed up in the kitchen cooking and crying. When we sat down to eat, she said how she could feel that any day now she would die and that we should be prepared for it. Which then made my mom cry at the thought.

When Abuela did die, I didn't cry.

When Dad got sick, I didn't have time to cry. Had to make sure Jules made it to class on time and sober. Make sure that Mom ate while she lived in the hospital with Dad. Make sure we could afford the mortgage that Dad left us with because he could no longer work. When he died, truthfully, I was relieved at his suffering being over but then I still couldn't cry because I had to make sure that Mom didn't follow him quickly after.

I cried when Jules left for school though. Surprised the hell outta me. But as her car rounded the end of our block the tears came pouring out.

Mom was also bawling and she looked at me.

Pensava que odiavas tu hermanita. *[I thought you hated your little sister.]*

Claro que no mama, tu sabes que amo a mi hermana. *[Oh come on Mom, you know I love my sister.]*

Ah intonces lloras por que la vas a extranyar. Vas a estar triste de no tiener la cerca. *[Oh well then you're crying 'cause you're going to miss her. You're going to be sad 'cause you won't have her close.]*

No, no lloro por eso. *[No, no I'm not crying because of that.]*

No?

Lloro por que se que nunca mas va regrisar. Ella es muy especial para este pueblioto. Su vida queda lejos de aqui. *[I'm crying 'cause I know that she's never going to come back. She's too special for this little town. Her life is meant to be far from here.]*

My mom then took my hand in hers and we stood there a long time. Feeling the absence of a life without our Julia. I stood there and thought about when I was sixteen, the day I got my licence. I woke Julia up at 1 a.m. It was a cloudless night. We snuck out, pushed the truck down the block before starting it, and drove out to the lake. In the box of the truck, we lay in our sleeping bags, together, staring up at the dancing lights.

> ALICIA *looks up at the distorted northern lights. They are living, writhing through the sky. The world whips around and continues to spin till we are back inside Muffin Break.*

END OF ACT 1.

ACT TWO

SCENE 15: CLOSED UP

Nighttime. Muffin Break is closed, it's probably the way it will look from now on if CANDICE actually ever closes the shop down. Music is playing from the back. JULIA enters. She hears the music and makes her way to the counter. She knocks on it.

CANDICE: Give me a sec.

JULIA beats out the rhythm of the music on the counter. CANDICE enters. JULIA finally stops.

Fuck, you're so annoying.

JULIA: What? That's classic. Remember, we used to do that while Missy mopped up the IGA on Friday nights.

CANDICE: I remember we almost got her fired.

JULIA: What? She never told me that.

CANDICE: Probably 'cause if she did, ya would have kept doing it, just to see if ya could get 'er fired.

JULIA: You're probably right. I was a fucking jerk back then sometimes.

CANDICE: Most times.

JULIA: Fuck you.

CANDICE: Don't hate the truth speakers.

JULIA: I know it's not an excuse but I was drinking a lot back then.

CANDICE: We all were. Small town, nothing else fur teens ta do.

JULIA: But it went beyond that. I just wanted to obliterate my mind all the time.

CANDICE: Well of course.

JULIA: What do you mean of course?

CANDICE: Well, with all that fucking shit going on with your dad getting sick and all, who wouldn't want some control in their life.

JULIA: But when I drank that much, I didn't have control of anything.

CANDICE: You controlled how much you drank.

JULIA: Did I though?

CANDICE: Fuck yah, ya did. It's not like you were coming to school plastered or failing classes.

JULIA: I guess.

CANDICE: Look, I am not trying to minimize alcoholism or anything. Lord knows I have seen what it can do to a family around here. And sure, you were drinking a lot more than any of us were, but I bet you don't drink like that anymore, do you?

JULIA: Noooo!

CANDICE: There ya fucking go. Ya learned. Ya grew. And now look, you're a fucking MLA for fuck's sake.

JULIA: Thanks.

CANDICE: Now have a drink.

CANDICE pulls out a case of beer.

JULIA: Seriously!

CANDICE: What? We're adults now, we know how to drink in moderation.

JULIA: Fine. Do you think the liquor store is still open? I don't really drink beer anymore. I'll run and go grab something.

CANDICE: No need, my friend. Wasn't too sure whatcha drink these days so I picked up some options.

> *CANDICE pulls out bottles of red and white wine. She pulls out some premixed cocktails, a bottle of rum, vodka, and gin. She also pulls out some limes and lemons and mix to go with all the hard liquor.*

JULIA: CANDICE!

CANDICE: We're not going to drink it all, was just tryin' tah be a good host.

JULIA: Much appreciated. I'll have some red wine, thank you.

CANDICE: Coming right up.

JULIA: So what do you wanna get for dinner?

CANDICE: Oh I already ordered.

JULIA: From where?

CANDICE: Dragon of course.

JULIA: Nice. Wait, I'm vegetarian.

CANDICE: I know. I read that interview you did about how we can all make a green impact.

JULIA: You read that?

CANDICE: Jules, of course.

JULIA: I can't believe you read that.

CANDICE: Believe it!

> GREG *walks into the store with a paper bag of food and something else under his arm.*

GREG: Hello hello! I've got a Chinese food delivery for Candice! Is there a Candice at this address?

CANDICE: Oh fuck off, G-Money, and get in here.

GREG: Hi, Julia!

JULIA: Hi, Greg.

GREG: How ya doing?

JULIA: I'm all right. You?

GREG: I'm good thanks. You all checked in to the hotel?

JULIA: Yeah.

GREG: How was the drive up?

JULIA: Uh it was good.

GREG: I don't know if I could do that anymore.

CANDICE: What're you talkin' 'bout? You drove to Manitoba and back last summer.

GREG: Yah but that was for vacation not for work.

JULIA: Visiting family in Manitoba?

GREG: Nope. Just never seen anything past Edmonton so I went, I saw, then turned 'round, came back. It was great!

CANDICE: You're so weird.

JULIA: Greg, how did you know that I drove up and that I was staying at the hotel?

GREG: How do you think? Melissa stopped by the restaurant to pick up her lunch for work and we got to chatting, told me you just rolled in. Then your sister came by with the girls for dinner and was yapping at me 'bout how she can't believe you're wasting your money on a hotel in yur hometown.

CANDICE: Small town, fast news, Jules.

GREG: You betcha.

JULIA: I didn't know Dragon Palace delivered. Is that something that the new management has implemented?

GREG: New management? I wish. Even though I run the place now, my dad comes in every Sunday to see how we handle the after-church rush.

CANDICE: Just tell him to be retired! Go on vacation!

GREG: Yah right, his vacation is coming in and telling me he did it better.

JULIA: Your dad does not change.

GREG: Nope. I can just imagine what he would say if I wanted to offer delivery. "Why would we deliver? We have the restaurant. They can come here and get the food hot or take it home if they want!"

CANDICE: Then I feel extra special for being your only delivery ever.

GREG: Yah well since I knew Julia was here, I figured I'd come say hi. Also this came back from the engravers.

GREG takes the thing from under his arm and begins to unwrap it.

CANDICE: Oh it's finally ready!

GREG: Took them long enough. I still can't believe they spelt yur name wrong the first time. How long ya lived here?

CANDICE: My whole life!

GREG: Yah. So embarrassing. On behalf of town council, for your many years of service and support to our community. I present to you, the first ever citizen excellence award.

GREG gives the plaque to CANDICE. JULIA applauds.

JULIA: Congratulations! That's so great, Candice!

CANDICE: Yah yah yah. Thanks, G. Thank you, Jules, for the applause.

GREG & JULIA: Speech! Speech!

CANDICE: *(clearing her throat)* Fuck off!

They all laugh.

GREG: Hey, Jules, I'm excited about our meeting tomorrow.

JULIA: Our meeting?

GREG: With town council.

JULIA: You'll be there?

GREG: I am a town councillor.

JULIA: So then you'll be at that meeting.

GREG: It is with town council.

JULIA: Great.

GREG: I'm interested to know what news you bring from this new government that warranted a face-to-face meeting with the parliamentary secretary. Wanna give me a sneak peek?

JULIA: Umm it's probably best to wait for tomorrow. That way council can hear the info together and we can discuss any questions you all may have at the same time.

GREG: Sure...

CANDICE: Stop it, both of you. No more work talk. Yur not sweating it out in the kitchen, Jules is in town for a few days, and Muffin Break is closed, for now, soon for good. Let's just have a few, okay? Greg, what do ya want?

GREG: I'll take a Pils. Thanks.

CANDICE: You want a top-up?

JULIA: I'm still good, thanks.

GREG: So when do you head out, Jules?

CANDICE: Jeezuz, she just got here, G!

GREG: What? I wanna know how much time we have her here for.

JULIA: I head back Monday.

GREG: That's plenty a' time.

JULIA: Well not really. I have meetings in the area every day till then.

GREG: Wow they're working you hard, aren't they?

CANDICE: Like a dog.

JULIA: It's good though. It means they see potential in me. I'm one of the youngest in the party and I plan to serve for a long time. Being the Parliamentary Secretary for Environmental Industry Reform means I get to have more face time like this with constituents, and bring that all back to the Minister. I get to be in the legislature instead of on the lawn protesting. And as a bonus, a task like this will probably set me up nicely for a cabinet position down the road where I'll get to call some shots on policy.

GREG: They tell ya that?

JULIA: Not in so many words but it's a logical path. A lot of folks who go on to be ministers work as parliamentary secretaries at some point. This will get me some experience under my belt to know how I can become a better leader within the party.

CANDICE: Damn, Jules! Listen to you. I've never knew you to have such . . . ambitions.

JULIA: Neither did I! I honestly thought I would have had to come back here once I finished school but I got really into activism and volunteering. Then I got involved in politics, which just felt right so I kept going.

GREG: Well you're really involved now.

JULIA: It's all because I really care about the work we're doing, and plan tah do. Beautiful British Columbia's always been in the pocket of one industry or another. It's really going to be different from here on out.

GREG: It has been different. We've been struggling to adjust at the district level. And then a lot of folks left when the pipeline did. Not to mention local business might not survive any drastic changes to industry in this town.

JULIA: You might not survive the fire that's on your doorstep now. You can't be afraid of change.

GREG: I am not afraid of change, Jules, and it's not what "might" happen. The Peace Country has already seen negative effects from day one of the BCEA taking charge. Muffin Break is one of those.

CANDICE: That's not fair, Greg. This shop was on its way out long before.

GREG: But they sure as shit didn't help your situation.

CANDICE: You wanna fucking know what really didn't help my situation? Giving the all clear for a Tim Hortons franchise to be erected two fucking blocks from the only other coffee shop in town.

GREG: I know, Candice, you've spoken to council before.

CANDICE: I'm not fucking speaking to council now, am I? I'm fucking talking to my friend.

GREG: Well why don't you say something new instead of your tired old fucking speech about big franchises.

CANDICE: You fucking little shit!

GREG's cellphone goes off.

GREG: Go for Greg. No, now's fine. Okay yah, I understand. Yup, I can come straight from Muffin Break.

>*GREG hangs up.*

I have tah go. Thanks for the beer, Candice.

CANDICE: You didn't even open it.

JULIA: Fire in the kitchen?

GREG: No. That wasn't the restaurant. It was the station.

CANDICE: Go then. Quick.

GREG: Thanks, I'll fill you both in later once I know more.

CANDICE: Okay.

>*GREG leaves.*

JULIA: The station?

CANDICE: Fire station. Greg's the captain of the volunteer force.

JULIA: Busy guy.

CANDICE: You know it.

>*A red light flashes in the windows of Muffin Break.*

JULIA: I hope everything is okay.

CANDICE: The way he ran out of here, more'n likely something to do with the fire. Last summer we were on and off evac notice for 'bout eight weeks straight. Had poor Greg run ragged every time the notice got updated.

JULIA: Shit, do you think we need to be concerned?

CANDICE: Nah, I'm sure he's just getting an update from forestry services. If we were on evac notice we'd be getting a text on all our phones.

They check their phones.

JULIA: Candice...

CANDICE: 'Sup?

JULIA: I'm really impressed by you two.

CANDICE: Thanks?

JULIA: No seriously. You two care a lot for this town.

CANDICE: Of course we do. This is our home. No government has really given two shits about us except when we make the news for a natural disaster. Okay enough of that. Let's drink to the Muffin Break.

CANDICE raises her drink.

JULIA: And to you and your award!

JULIA raises her glass.

CANDICE: Thanks.

They cheers. The past comes drifting onto the stage as we are transported to their teenage years once again.

SCENE 16: AT THE PARTY

We are out at Long Road. A dusty, well-worn spot that has seen generations of teens obliterate themselves every weekend. They all arrive at the party except for ALICIA. We hear some hard '70s rock blasting from a truck.

MELISSA: What?! They haven't lit the fire yet?

CANDICE: Of course not.

GREG: I mean, they've been out here for an hour, what's the holdup?

CANDICE: They only have so many pallets. I figure they wanna wait'll more folks show up.

GREG: But aren't most folks driving around till they light the fire?

CANDICE: Yup.

GREG: So if they light the fire, people will come.

CANDICE: Maybe.

GREG: So then they should light the fire.

CANDICE: But people still might not come?

GREG: Why wouldn't they come?

MELISSA: They could go to a house party?

GREG: But everyone we talked to said that was a no go.

JULIA: People change their minds.

CANDICE: It is a wee bit cold tonight.

GREG: Then it stands to reason that we should light the fire!

MELISSA: Stands to reason?

CANDICE & JULIA: *(playfully mocking GREG)* Stands to reason, my good sir!

CANDICE: *(to the other teens waiting for the fire to be lit)* You there, boy, the fire. Attend to it!

JULIA: Chip chop chip!

GREG: You two are hilarious.

MELISSA: You should see them with a substitute teacher.

GREG: Oh I can picture it. I bet it's a real vaudeville show.

CANDICE & JULIA: Vaudeville!

JULIA: What da fuck is that?

CANDICE: I don' fucking know, but whatever it is, deserves a shot.

(pulls a mickey from her back pocket) Greggie, that how you talk in the big city?

GREG: Like what?

JULIA: You know, talking all stands to reason, vaudeville and shit.

CANDICE: I thought you'd come back from Van all hood.

GREG: Yah, right. That's me.

JULIA: Waddaya mean? G looks so gangster.

GREG: Fuck off!

They all laugh.

CANDICE: But seriously, G, this is how it goes every weekend.

MELISSA: Well since we started boozing and cruising and not hoofing it 'round town with beers in our backpacks.

GREG: Then I haven't missed much, have I?

MELISSA: Nope.

GREG: And are there always enough pallets in town to burn?

CANDICE: Yup.

MELISSA: Not always.

CANDICE: Right.

MELISSA: One time we were running low on pallets, so we burnt a washing machine.

GREG: Why a washing machine?

MELISSA: Because it was here. Someone musta dumped it. So we burnt it.

CANDICE: Burnt is a strong word. It mostly just warped and melted.

GREG: Yur shitting me?

JULIA: No. It's right over there if you wanna take a look.

JULIA points to the husk of a washing machine somewhere off stage.

MELISSA: Okay there's gotta be enough of us here now. Candice, say something.

CANDICE: You say something.

MELISSA: Fuck that.

JULIA shouts to the folks lighting the fire.

JULIA: Yo what's the fuckin' hold up, quit playing with your fuckin' peckers and fuckin' light the fuckin' pallets already.

CANDICE: You, madam, are pure class.

ALICIA walks on stage.

ALICIA: Yah, fuck you too buddy! Come 'ere and say that! I'll rip yur tongue outta yur fucking mouth and make ya lick your own fucking asshole with it.

CANDICE: I see it runs in the family.

MELISSA: Yur not even drinkin'.

ALICIA: So?

JULIA: Don't get in a fight.

ALICIA: Try an' stop me, I'll fight if I fucking want to. Sober or drunk.

JULIA: Oh yur so fucking tuff.

ALICIA: Keep going, I'll knock your fucking teeth out as well.

CANDICE: Holy shit ladies! It's waaaaay too early for a family fist fight.

JULIA: Wouldn't be much of a fight.

ALICIA: Yah I'd put you down pretty fuckin' quick bud.

MELISSA: Jezuz are all you Mexicans always this angry?

> *They all pause and turn to look at* MELISSA. *She takes a swig of her beer, cool as cucumber.*

JULIA: *(shocked)* Missy!

ALICIA: What did you say, pukey pants?

GREG: She asked, are all you Mexicans this angry?

CANDICE: Oh shit!

ALICIA: Say it again.

MELISSA: Are all you Mexicans this angry?

> MELISSA *bolts off stage.* ALICIA *runs after her.*

ALICIA: Get the fuck back here, Melissa!

GREG: Shit! Is Missy gunna be all right?

JULIA: Oh yah. Al knows it's a joke. I think.

> *There is a big whoosh as someone throws gas on the fire. We are blinded by the flare of light. As the bonfire burns it transforms into the Jackfish Lake fire, still burning uncontrollably.*

SCENE 17: INUNDATION

The fire is raging now. Smoke fills the space. The only thing standing in its way are the forest firefighters. We hear the crackle and hums of chatter on CB radios, helicopters flying overhead, and water planes whooshing by. The sound of the fire is like a freight train as we are in the heart of it. On the CB radios we hear:

VOICE 1: This was all fine when we drove out here four hours ago.

VOICE 2: It got away from us two hours ago.

VOICE 3: It's heading back up toward town.

VOICE 1: This thing is just ripping now—

VOICE 2: This fire is starting to bump the road east ah here, you guys heading out yet?

VOICE 3: I think we can catch it—

VOICE 1: You reckon?—

VOICE 3: I mean we got 400 gallons, couple bladder bags.

VOICE 4: Engine 341 where you at?— You need to start rolling out, are you in section seven yet?— Do you copy?— Engine 341 are you in section seven yet? Do you copy?

VOICE 2: Copy. It's heading north as well.

VOICE 1: North?— We need to also head south. Towards town.

VOICE 4: Crews are heading that way—keep pushing through.

VOICE 1: I thought this thing was close to being contained?

VOICE 3: Initial attack crews thought so too but those high winds last night had other plans.

VOICE 2: Let the mayor know it's time to be on evacuation notice and start the voluntary evacuations.

VOICE 4: They're informed.

VOICE 1: Copy that, looks like we are cut off now, going to double back.

The flames are moving like liquid mercury across the stage.

On the edge of the smoke something comes into view. It is the northern lights. They are not as strong as they could be but they are there illuminating GREG.

GREG: I moved back home after graduating from university and started working for my parents. This one time, after we had closed up the restaurant for the night, my dad waved me over to sit with him in one of the booths. He had poured some whisky for the two of us. Not an unusual occurrence but instead of swigging it back while we scraped the grills we sat in that booth. After a few sips he asked me why I had moved back. I said it was to help him and Mom out while I saved up some cash, pay off my student loans. That maybe once that's done I'll head back to the city but only if he and Mom were doing okay. He just sat there nodding, taking sips of his whisky, and then bluntly told me that I better not be thinking of spending the rest of my life behind the grill. Because that was never their plan for me. Once they got too old, they planned to sell or close up. This was never meant to be for me. This restaurant was not meant to be our family's legacy. I was.

He then got up. Patted me on the shoulder and began walking back towards the kitchen and as he turned on the kitchen radio he said, "This town doesn't appreciate who you are. What you can do. You should go do better than this, somewhere else." And then began his nightly ritual of mopping.

I sat there dumbfounded, thinking how my dad of all people could say that. They were the ones who moved here. Who risked everything to come to a town half a world away from all things familiar to them. Where we were the only Asians. Where we stood out all the time and part of me hated them for that, for settling here. In the middle of fucking nowhere. Because they always told me to be on my best behaviour, at all times, 'cause everything I did wrong was setting the standard of what Chinese people were like around the world. Even though until we finally got high-speed internet up here all people knew of "China" was chop suey and Jackie Chan movies.

It didn't help that instead of getting to do what other kids in town were doing, like swimming lessons and sleepovers, I was bussing tables or folding takeout menus. Aside from school, I was lucky if I got to see my friends outside of the restaurant. So of course, as a teenager, when I got the littlest morsel of freedom, I started to party, hard. Not any different than most teens 'round here but I was out to prove I belonged with everyone here. Most weekends I could hide it from my parents. Until I didn't. Maybe they thought by sending me away I would fall in love with the big city and stay there. That I would hate them enough to never wanna be like them. Instead of running back because as it turns out, it scared me more to fade into the crowd than to stick out like a sore thumb.

Maybe Dad was right. Maybe I should have tried harder to do better than this, somewhere else. Because no matter what I try to do no one wants to hear it. Folks think that if they just stick to their guns everything will be fine. That what's worked for the last fifty years, will work for the next fifty. Not fuckin' likely an' we're just going to become another ghost town when it all comes crumbling down around us.

> *The northern lights swell and light the space. As they fade, the past comes back to us. It drifts onto the space as* GREG *watches. A vehicle rolls up, we hear it idle, a door opens, music plays through the open door.*

SCENE 19: THE AFTER-PARTY

We are outside Muffin Break. It's closed now since it's long past its operating hours. The kids enter as the truck is turned off.

MELISSA: *(singing)* "Whoa, Black Betty! Blam-ba-lam. Whoa, Black Betty, ramble jam!"

CANDICE: That's not how the song goes!

MELISSA: How the fuck do you know? The guy mumbles so much it's anyone's guess.

JULIA: Fair 'nough, but I'm pretty sure "ramble jam" isn't one of the lyrics.

GREG: I dunno, it really does sound like ramble jam.

MELISSA: See, I'm not the only one.

CANDICE: Wow two whole people.

MELISSA: Yah and we know the truth!

JULIA: As if!

ALICIA: Okay, dorks, it's 3 a.m. Imma drive y'all home.

JULIA: Oh come on, Al. Let's do a few more loser laps! I still have some whisky left.

(pulls out a mickey of whisky) See!

ALICIA: Are you forgetting that we have to go with Mom to church in the morning?

JULIA: Pffff! No problem. I go all the time after partying.

ALICIA: But if you finish that whisky, yur gunna wake up drunk.

JULIA: Even better, church goes so much faster when yur drunk.

ALICIA: Whatever, I'm tired.

JULIA: Lame!

> *Others join her and call out "Lame!"*

ALICIA: Y'all exhaust me.

GREG: We're super thankful for you driving us, Al.

MELISSA: Yah! And we can walk home from uptown so go to bed.

CANDICE: Oh fur sure!

JULIA: Yah we'll walk from here.

ALICIA: You better be ready to go when Mom is.

JULIA: Always am!

ALICIA: All right get home safe you guys.

JULIA: Oh shit!

> *ALICIA goes to leave but JULIA hears a song from ALICIA's car and runs past her off stage to turn it up. Once it's loud she runs back on stage.*

Before you go let's just dance to this song! Please please please!

ALICIA: Jules . . .

JULIA: Come on!

JULIA pulls ALICIA back to the group.

MELISSA: Yah, Al, just let loose. You didn't get to drink but at least you can dance!

CANDICE: Just let all that pent-up party in you out. Dance with us!

GREG: Do it!

ALICIA: Fine!

They all begin to dance, until we hear the whoop of the RCMP and see the lights of their squad car.

MELISSA: Oh fuck!

ALICIA: It's fine, they probably want us to turn down the music. Don't give them a reason to get out of the car, Julia.

JULIA: It was one time.

ALICIA: Two times.

JULIA: Two times.

CANDICE: That she knows of.

ALICIA: Hide the fucking booze!

MELISSA: Got it.

GREG: I'll hide it in my stomach.

CANDICE: Fly at it, G-Money, but don't let them see you do it. They'll dump it all and then take ya home in the back of the car. Try explaining that one to your dad.

GREG: Maybe I'll just leave this here then.

GREG puts a bottle of beer down.

Oh look someone littered and left this bottle right here. What a bad person. This should go in the recycle bin.

JULIA: Fuck that! They know we all drink underage. They should just let us have our fun.

CANDICE: Jules.

ALICIA: Get her mickey.

JULIA: Don't fucking touch me. I'm fine.

MELISSA: Just give it to your sister. She can just say it's hers.

JULIA: Why are all of you sooo worried. S'like nunya evr gotten a free ride home buhfore.

GREG: I haven't.

MELISSA: None of us have.

CANDICE: Except Jules.

ALICIA: For fuck's sake, Julia. Stop acting like a spoiled brat and give me the goddamn mickey!!!

JULIA finishes the rest of her mickey of whisky.

JULIA: There ya go.

(to the police off stage) Hey, pigs, how'd ya like them apples! Impressive, no? Finished it in one go. Come get me! I'd like my free ride home. I don't trust my DD anymore. Or you can try and round up my friends here. They could use a ride as well.

> *Everyone goes running off stage except for ALICIA and JULIA.*

GREG: Fuck!

MELISSA: Fuck, Jules!

CANDICE: You fucking idiot!

ALICIA: Yur a real piece of fucking work, Jules.

> *The northern lights burst onto the scene as ALICIA and JULIA look at each other. It washes over them. They recognize each other through the flow of time. Then ALICIA leaves.*

The northern lights shine in the sky so well. They hug us. Their cosmic dance makes us feel the sheer scope of what it is to be small in the universe. We are all specs of dust in a grand ocean of black.

JULIA: Choices have consequences. Sometimes we are free to make those choices and sometimes the consequence of someone else's choice is thrust upon us. Like how my parents had to deal with how hard it was to immigrate here in the '70s. They chose to leave their families back in Guatemala—and I was stuck with the consequences of growing up without my abuelos. My parents couldn't afford for us to go back regularly and chose to send money to help instead of spending it on a family holiday. As my abuelos passed away, my parents could only afford for one of them to go attend the funeral, while the other stayed with us. The consequences of working a blue-collar job that doesn't afford you four round-trip tickets to your own parent's funeral.

As a kid, I would pester my dad to tell me about his days as a youth back home. What was he like? What was Mom like? What could ever make you decide to leave a tropical paradise? He was such a patient man and would answer in his devilish way. "Oh, mija, I was very poor but very handsome. Your mom was the most beautiful woman in the neighbourhood, cars would stop in the street for her. I will tell you why when you are old enough to understand what it really means to be Indigenous in a tropical paradise." He never told me that last one though, he got sick and all his experiences, his stories, became trapped in his mind as a result.

After my father passed, after they lowered his body into the ground, I was sitting on the couch with my mom, sitting in silence with the fact that Dad was gone. It was so quiet that I heard my tears fall onto my lap before I even noticed that I was crying. My mother placed her hand on mine and told me, "Mija, no llores. Era su tiempo y trabjó tan duro toda su vida y sufrío tanto. Ahora puede descansar en paz." [*"Don't cry, mija. It was his time and he worked hard his whole life, suffered so much. He can rest in peace now."*]

I told her that wasn't why I was crying. I was crying because I was so sorry that my life choices had taken me away from them, from Alicia, from everything I knew my whole life. That I wasn't around when he died, that I barely came back now and that I had missed so much. That I had left because I felt that this wasn't where I needed to be because my family never understood who I really was. And that I never felt like I was really a part of what they shared. That this town was suffocating me. That I couldn't be more than the Julia everyone knew and grew up with. And that her and Dad were probably disappointed in the fact that I choose to make my life far from theirs.

She then gave me the biggest hug of my life and said, "Mija, don't be stupid. You are just doing the same as we did. You have chosen to take the same path of striking out on your own to find what calls you. We came here, so that you could have that option. If you are happy with what you have chosen to do with your life, then so are we. We are so proud of you."

We sit with JULIA for a while and allow her to breathe. The northern lights dance. The present begins to shove its way onto the stage as day breaks. It is a dusty, saturated orange that fills the sky.

SCENE 21: OUCH

We are out front of the Muffin Break. JULIA sits with her head in her hands. CANDICE comes out from the back with a cup of coffee. She hands it to JULIA.

CANDICE: Drink up.

JULIA: Oh god. Did hangovers always hurt this much?

CANDICE: Are you really that hungover?

JULIA: Yes! Aren't you?

CANDICE: I've got a bit of dry mouth.

JULIA: That's so unfair.

CANDICE: You're the one who stopped drinking like we used to. Yur body's gone soft.

JULIA: No one should drink like we used to.

CANDICE: I suppose. What time's yur meeting?

JULIA: Nine.

CANDICE: Oh ya got plenty of time to pop an Advil and grab a catnap in yur hotel room.

JULIA: I wish. I have to check in with my office before I head to council and I still need to go over my notes.

CANDICE: Then you shoulda had a little less tah drink then.

JULIA: I'm going to fucking kill you!

JULIA goes to get up.

Ow, ow, ow.

CANDICE: Serves ya right. I was only being a gracious host last night.

JULIA: I'm so thankful.

A truck pulls up. MELISSA comes on stage.

MELISSA: What the fuck are you two doing out here at 5 a.m.?

JULIA: Good morning to you too.

MELISSA: Ouff, Jules, you look like shit.

CANDICE: She's hungover.

MELISSA: You went to the pub without me?

CANDICE: You were working, remember?

MELISSA: Right. Still would have been nice to be invited.

JULIA: We can have a drink this weekend.

MELISSA: Yes!

JULIA: I'll also invite Greg at our meeting today.

MELISSA: Yur meetin'! Right! I don't think it's going to happen. Half the council is on the fire department so there's really not anyone to have a meeting with.

JULIA: What are you talking about?

MELISSA: Have you not checked your phones yet today?

CANDICE: Mine's dead, charging inside.

MELISSA: Greg sent you a text. Fire's gotten real close to West Fraser. Greg and the rest of the fire department went out there to help stay ahead of the fire, soak everything down. Alicia's got her crews there digging some trenches. Don't be surprised if we're put on evac notice with the fire that close to the mill.

CANDICE: If that goes up it's gunna rip right into the gully and then straight through town here in no time.

MELISSA: Oh fur sure.

JULIA: Wait, why is the town's volunteer fire department dealing with the forest fire?

MELISSA: If we waited for the forest guys to make their way over there'd be nothin' left.

CANDICE: Meanwhile we're gunna do anything we can to help. They have their hands full. I'm sure it's appreciated.

MELISSA: All right, I'm outta here, I was able to grab a couple hours of sleep after work so I'm gunna head back out there and help. Call if you need anything.

CANDICE: Yah for sure.

MELISSA leaves.

JULIA: Holy shit.

CANDICE: Yah.

Beat.

Hey, go back to your hotel and get ready to hit the road. Call your sister to make sure she doesn't need help with the girls or something.

JULIA: That's a good idea.

CANDICE: If you need me I'll be inside doing the same thing.

> *JULIA watches her go. She looks around. Checks her phone and scrolls with some intention. Time begins to melt again. Floating on the current of memory JULIA sits, contemplating. The past washes over JULIA.*

SCENE 22: DINNER TIME

We are taken back to the summer. It has gotten late in the day, but up North days are long in the summer. We hear country music being played. Probably from someone working on their truck in the neighbourhood. The kids come back on stage with slushie cups. Except for GREG, who stays standing next to his bike, looking around.

JULIA: Oh yah, that's the stuff!

ALICIA: Disgusting.

JULIA: What?

ALICIA: You put all the flavours in there.

JULIA: Yah. That's the best!

ALICIA: Weirdo.

CANDICE: Well, what did you get?

ALICIA: Coke.

CANDICE: Just Coke?

ALICIA: Yah.

CANDICE: Laaame.

ALICIA: Oh and yours is so exciting?

CANDICE: You know it! Watermelon Sprite.

ALICIA: Oh wow two flavours, so fancy.

CANDICE: It is fancy, you have to layer the watermelon in very carefully so that you get the flavour mix just right. You can't just go half and half. First you gotta make sure that the bottom layers are not as thick as the top layers. You know, those melt faster, since your hands hold the cup there. Then as you fill it up you make thicker layers so that as it melts, you still have some separation. That way every once and awhile you get a swig of just Sprite or just watermelon. And then you also get Sprite watermelon flavour. So it's like three slushies in one.

They all stare at CANDICE.

JULIA: I just like all the flavours and hate choosing. Simple.

ALICIA: You are simple.

JULIA: Al!

ALICIA: You really put that much thought into your slushies?

CANDICE: Slushies are serious business, Al.

ALICIA: Not really.

CANDICE: You wouldn't understand.

ALICIA: Try me.

MELISSA: Ah! Brain freeze! Ow, ow, ow!

JULIA: Stop drinking it then!

CANDICE: No drink more! That will stop it.

ALICIA: What?! Who told you that?

CANDICE: That's what my cousins say to me!

MELISSA: Uggggh . . .

ALICIA: Those losers?

CANDICE: It works for me!

GREG: Put your tongue on the roof of your mouth. Like this.

> GREG *shows* MELISSA.

MELISSA: *(with her tongue on the roof of her mouth)* Wha-owww. It's working!

JULIA: Hey! How did you know that?

GREG: My dad.

CANDICE: Smart man.

GREG: And a mean man, so can we get going back.

MELISSA: Where's your slushie?

GREG: I drank it.

CANDICE: That was fast.

GREG: I'm not supposed to be uptown, remember? So if my dad drove by and saw us or if I came home with a slushie cup he would know where I was.

CANDICE: Well I can't ride with one hand so I'm not going anywhere.

JULIA: I can, I just don't want to.

ALICIA: It's so warm today, maybe I'll take a nap.

GREG: Come on. I'll leave.

ALICIA: Not without your babysitter you won't.

CANDICE: Yah what if your dad sees you riding all alone.

MELISSA: You wouldn't let him leave would you, Alicia?

ALICIA: I'll sit on him if I have to.

GREG: Then hurry up!

> *ALICIA's phone rings. It is one of the old '90s Motorola-style flip phones that has an antenna to extend. She answers it and begins to walk away.*

ALICIA: Hola, Mamá. No todo vía estamos con sus amigas. Sí. Estamos cerca de la casa. Unos cinco minutos. *[Hi, Mom. No, we are still hanging out with her friends. Yes. We're close to the house. Like five minutes.]*

MELISSA: Is that your mom?

JULIA: How many Spanish people do you know that live here?

CANDICE: Wow, chill Julia.

MELISSA: Well, I don't know many folks in town yet so . . .

GREG: Don't worry, that won't take long.

CANDICE: Yah! There's barely anyone here anyways.

JULIA: And we're the only ones you need to know in our grade.

> *ALICIA comes back on stage.*

ALICIA: Great, well Mom says dinner is ready and that I should get you dorks to your homes. Come on.

GREG: Yes! About time.

GREG takes off.

ALICIA: Wait for us, Greg.

ALICIA goes to her bike.

CANDICE: Don't worry, Al, I'll catch him.

CANDICE goes get her bike and takes off after GREG.

ALICIA: Better you than me. Greg, you're going to get me in trouble! Get back here!

ALICIA takes off.

JULIA: Come on, Missy, if you fall behind you're gunna get lost in the gully.

MELISSA: Hey, Julia.

JULIA: Sup?

MELISSA: Do you not like me?

JULIA: Why would you ask that? Of course I like you.

MELISSA: Like do you not want me around?

JULIA: What?

MELISSA: Well, um, you keep saying that you're gunna leave me in the gully and stuff.

JULIA: Oh.

MELISSA: Yah it kinda hurts my feelings.

JULIA: I'm sorry.

ALICIA comes back on stage.

ALICIA: Come on, you two! Let's go.

JULIA: Missy, you wanna come for dinner?

MELISSA: For real?

JULIA: Yah! Come on!

ALICIA: I would ask Mom first.

MELISSA: Oh yah, if it's okay with your parents.

JULIA: My mom won't care.

ALICIA: Are you sure about that?

JULIA: ¿Crees que le va importar? *[Do you think she'll care?]*

ALICIA: Vos sabes que a ella no le guasta tener visita sin aviso primero. *[You know she doesn't like to have company without being told first.]*

JULIA: Pero es mi amiga no es visita. *[But she's my friend not company.]*

ALICIA: Whatever, it's your funeral if you don't ask Mom. And why do you have to speak Spanish? You sound disabled.

JULIA: You don't own Spanish, Alicia!!

ALICIA: No but I do know how to speak it.

ALICIA leaves.

JULIA: Ahhh! I hate you!

MELISSA: I'm sorry if coming for dinner is going to make trouble. I can just go home.

JULIA: No, it's fine. Alicia's just being a jerk.

MELISSA: I didn't know you could also speak Spanish.

JULIA: I normally don't. Especially with my sister.

MELISSA: Oh.

JULIA: I only speak it with my mom, really.

MELISSA: Why does Alicia say that you sound disabled?

JULIA: Ugh, I have an accent.

MELISSA: I can't tell.

JULIA: No, in Spanish, and I don't know as many words as Al since she's from Guatemala.

MELISSA: Really?

JULIA: Yup. My dad says, "You're our New World baby, and Al's our Third World baby." Whatever that means.

MELISSA doesn't get the joke. JULIA, looking to keep her interested, looks around for ALICIA.

Can I tell you one thing but you can never tell Al I told you?

MELISSA: Sure.

JULIA: Well she may say I sound disabled when I speak Spanish but at least I didn't fail kindergarten for not being able to speak English. (*laughs*)

MELISSA: She failed kindergarten?!?!

JULIA: Shhh!! Yah. But don't ever say anything, 'cause she will kick your ass.

MELISSA: Oh okay.

ALICIA: (*off stage*) Julia! Melissa! Move it!

> *The girls get on their bikes and go. The evening sound of summer fills our ears once again. Slowly the day corrodes into orange. It has gotten insidiously smokey.*

SCENE 23: HELPING OUT

We are back outside the Muffin Break. The fire has come very close to town. Close enough that the sun's rays are blocked from fully reaching the earth and washing us all in a glow we know all too well now.

GREG: Candice, thanks again for helping out.

CANDICE: No prob. Glad I can still be useful.

MELISSA: Oh come on, C. You're not just the Muffin Break.

ALICIA: You sure you're all good with leaving West Fraser to the forestry folks, G?

GREG: Not my circus, not my monkeys. BC Wildfire Services wants tah run the show, they can. They're trained for it. I'll be here in town making sure we save as much as we can.

ALICIA: Did you see how tired they looked? I do not envy them.

MELISSA: Yah it's a tough fuckin' gig, wildfire crew. They're really givin' it their all. Just fuckin' wish the weather would cooperate.

ALICIA: Yah, the winds really picked up which doesn't help.

GREG: Your family okay, C? Fires startin' tah get real close to the reserve out there.

CANDICE: Oh yah, Dad's not waiting to get the order to evacuate. He loaded up the horses and boarded up the house. Made his way to my auntie's property just outside Pouce Coupe this morning.

GREG: If the weather gives us a break, his house should be fine.

CANDICE: Fuck let's hope so. I'm gunna head out there and wet everything down as much as I can.

MELISSA: I'll join you once we get back from making sure most folks are getting ready tah clear out if we need to.

ALICIA: I can run one of my excavators out to your pops place and help too if ya like?

CANDICE: You sure, Al?

ALICIA: Of course. How 'bout you, G? You gunna come out there? Could use a pilot car driver to make it through this smoke.

GREG: I'll see how I'm feeling. I'm gunna get around to as many folks as possible before I fall into bed. I've been up since yesterday and I'm going to be pretty useless if I don't get sleep soon.

MELISSA: No shit. Why don't you go grab a couple winks now?

GREG: Maybe. Just wanna make sure everyone's taking evac notice seriously this time.

CANDICE: We've all become a bit numb to it now.

ALICIA: You betcha.

> *JULIA enters.*

CANDICE: Jules!

ALICIA: Where the hell are you coming from?

JULIA: I was taking calls.

ALICIA: You were taking calls in all of this?

JULIA: Yes. I was supposed to head out to Dawson later this afternoon but since the fire's blocked the road outta town that way, wasn't really a point to try.

ALICIA: I'm surprised the hotel let you stay. Whole town's been put on notice, non-residents are supposed to get outta here.

JULIA: They didn't. Been taking calls in my car.

ALICIA: Fuck you really love your job don'tcha?

JULIA: If only you knew. Where are the girls?

ALICIA: At their nana and papa's in Prince.

JULIA: Smart.

ALICIA: Didn't take much smarts to make that call.

CANDICE: You could've come here to take your meetings.

JULIA: Yeah these were not really anything I could do in public . . .

MELISSA: They know what's goin' on up 'ere, right?

JULIA: No they don't, they never will.

GREG: They gotta be pretty ignorant to not know our town might burn to the ground soon.

JULIA: I mean they know about the fire of course. I just . . . never mind.

MELISSA: Well, I'm not gunna complain that you're still here, we could use the help going door to door. You could jump in with me if ya like?

JULIA: I can't, sorry.

CANDICE: Why not?

JULIA: I have an emergency meeting with the Minister.

GREG: Now?

JULIA: Any minute now, I'm just waiting for a message from the Deputy Minister.

ALICIA: Then why the fuck did you come here, just so we know that you have a really important meeting?

JULIA: Because I didn't want to just text Candice, "Thanks for the booze last night, see ya in another ten years."

CANDICE: It's fine, Jules.

ALICIA: Bullshit.

JULIA: Excuse me?

ALICIA: You heard me. If this work trip hadn't come up we never woulda seen your face up here.

JULIA: The fuck do you know.

ALICIA: You've made it clear what happens here does not matter to you.

JULIA: Don't put words in my mouth.

ALICIA: You didn't even see Mom, did you?

MELISSA: Come on, you two. Shelf this for now.

CANDICE: For fuck's sake, ladies, this is not time for *Family Feud*.

JULIA: What makes you think I'm not trying to change what's going to happen here.

ALICIA: Gunna save us from the forest fire with your little meetings are you?

JULIA: I'm not talking about the fire, you idiot. I'm looking at what's going to be left after.

GREG: Does this have anything to do with the meeting we were supposed to have?

JULIA: Yes.

GREG: And?

JULIA: I'm not sure I can tell you, not until an official statement goes out at least.

GREG: Look, we knew that you were going to present the BCEA's Just Transition Plan and where exactly the Peace was included in that. What's changed?

JULIA: It's still all unfolding but it's looking like Suncor is backing out.

CANDICE: What?!

JULIA: Seems an unforeseen bottoming out of the price of crude is forcing them to scale back supporting an expansion into BC.

GREG: I fucking knew it! Once again we get fucked.

MELISSA: Jezuz. When is it a done deal?

JULIA: Tuesday. They're using all the coverage of the fires to squeak this under the radar. That's why I have to talk to the Minister before the cabinet meeting tomorrow morning.

CANDICE: So what, at least retraining is going to be funded. Just means moving out of the area for a bit.

JULIA: No.

ALICIA: Fuck off.

JULIA: If Suncor backs out there isn't enough for paid retraining. The BCEA is going to take the money from ending fossil fuel subsidies and partially carry out the transition. They'll bring in foreign skilled labour to bridge the gap till enough locals find the training.

CANDICE: Do you know what that means for towns like ours?

JULIA: Yes, of course I do. Better than anyone in the cabinet. If I can just get them to hear me out.

MELISSA: Did you know this was on the table?

JULIA: I knew it was a distant possibility.

ALICIA: And yet you came all the way up here, going town to town, telling us, "Don't worry, we got you."

JULIA: You think I would travel all the way up here knowing you're fucked and then ask to sit down with you and say don't worry. No. As much as you all wanna think that we can just do what we want as the government, greater forces are at play. Suncor only agreed 'cause they were getting exclusive rights to green energy development in the province. We had to guarantee them billions before we could get them to think about our future.

ALICIA: Don't kid yourself.

JULIA: Oh I'm not. I've been swallowing shit like this since joining the BCEA, being paraded out for the cameras, look at our young, Latina ex-activist. At least it's gotten me a seat at the table. I just thought this party would have more of a spine than the rest. Fuck.

GREG: Look don't beat yourself up over this, Jules. We're used to it. Government always thinks it knows best.

JULIA: That's why I have to stay and take this meeting. I want to help, but I'm better use on the phone than knocking door to door.

ALICIA: Jezuz fucking Christ, Jules. When the fuck did you stop givin' a shit about your home?

JULIA: Hometown. Get that through your fucking skull. And what good does having a hometown do any of us if we're all dead or displaced when the next season of forest fires hits.

ALICIA: Oh so you and your lot have it all figured out. Should we sit here waiting for a memo with a solution?

JULIA: I don't have anything figured out! I'm not you, miss always-had-it-together.

MELISSA: ENOUGH. We've wasted enough fuckin' time on this. Seems like no matter how much we hurt each other's feelings right now nothing is gunna fucking change the fact that hard times are here for us. When that fire comes screaming into this valley it's going to be a shit show. So we need to get out there and make sure folks are ready to hit the highway when we get the order to leave.

Jules, you're right you're gunna be pretty useless out there. We know this isn't your home anymore. But we also know that doesn't mean you don't care. We've got this. Don't feel guilty for doing what yur gut's telling you to do. Yur 'bout the only person who's stubborn enough to change their minds.

Snow begins to fall from the sky. They all look up. They wipe it off of themselves and stare in horror. It is snowing ash. It rains down on them. The sky has become more orange as well.

CANDICE: What the fuck?

JULIA: Ash?

GREG: Wind must have changed direction.

All of their cellphones go off almost all at once. They look at them and we can feel it sink in.

MELISSA: For fuck's sake, we can't catch a break.

CANDICE: You've gotta hit the highway, Jules.

JULIA: I have to give it five more minutes. I can't risk losing this call. I can't hit the road pretending that I don't see my hometown burning to the fucking ground in my rear-view mirror.

ALICIA: Then stay here as long as you want for fuck's sakes!

CANDICE: Jules, get going. Greg, where do you need us?

GREG: Candice, you can take the crown subdivision and, Al, you go to the Legion sub. You have fifteen minutes, you hear? Don't stop to argue, just make sure people are heading out.

MELISSA: I'll jump over to the rodeo grounds, make sure they got all the horses from the barns loaded up.

GREG: Got it. See ya, Jules.

MELISSA: Drive safe.

MELISSA and GREG leave.

ALICIA: Do what you want, Jules. But it's not worth risking your life to plead to people who have already made up their minds. I gotta head.

JULIA: Text me.

ALICIA: I will.

ALICIA leaves.

CANDICE: I gotta go help.

CANDICE leaves. JULIA's phone rings. JULIA stands there in the parking lot. She looks at her phone. The ash continues to snow on her building. The ash begins to cover us in the audience. JULIA's phone rings. She looks at it and then runs off. The sound of her ringer trails off.

SCENE 24: CONSUMPTION

The fire begins to grow again. It cracks as it consumes. It comes barreling down on us. Smoke pours in from the wings.

The world explodes into flame. We are left to sit in this crashing of natural disaster. A crimson reality of a future we are all complicit in if we allow it to happen. We sit helpless. As the fire begins to fade away we notice that all of the places that JULIA, ALICIA, CANDICE, MELISSA, *and* GREG *have gathered are glowing. We sit in silence for a time, witnessing.*

All lights snap off.

END OF PLAY.

ACKNOWLEDGEMENTS

I want to acknowledge that this play was written on the traditional and unceded lands of the xʷməθkwəy̓əm (Musqueam), Skwxwú7mesh (Squamish), Səl̓ílwətaɬ (Tsleil-Waututh), Qayqayt, Secwépemc, and the Syilx Okanagan Nations. It is with great privilege that I have been able to craft this story while traveling across these lands.

Thank you Kendra Fanconi for casting me in *Slime* and believing that interns could totally be in their mid-thirties. Thank you Bryony Lavery for writing such a beautiful play that inspired me to marry my activism, concern about the climate crisis, and playwriting together.

Thanks to Cory Philley and the Shadbolt Centre for the Arts who programmed us with only an idea and no script. Allowing us to produce a workshop full budget version was critical in this play's journey.

Infinite gratitude to Vicki Stroich, Estelle Shook, and everyone at the Caravan. Thank you for the gift of being invited to the National Playwrights Retreat. What a blessing that program is. So much love to my Caravan playwrights cohort, I couldn't have asked for a better group to share that time with.

An immense thank you to Donna Spencer and everyone at the Firehall. Your belief in this show means so much. Thank you Playwrights Theatre Centre for partnering with rice & beans on this play's development from concept to stage. Thanks to our other partners, VACT and the Push International Performance Festival. Your support has been invaluable to a small company like rice & beans.

There have been so many individuals who have given their time, energy and artistic talents to this project. I want to thank you all for collaborating with me on this journey. Thanks for going along with my hare-brained ideas or not shutting me down when I would jump up with fervent "I have an idea!" energy in the rehearsal room or when I would show up with entirely new scenes written between rehearsal days.

Endless gratitude to the team at rice & beans who produced both productions of this show. María Escolán, Cindy Kao, Howard Dai, and Karla Comanda. Especially Heather Barr who tirelessly campaigned for all of the artists and ensured that folks were well taken care of all while making sure the wheels didn't fall off the bus at rice & beans theatre.

Heidi, my dear Gemini sister, I am so grateful to have had you not only as my dramaturg on this project but also as one of the greatest mentors and champions I could ever ask for. Thank you for your endless encouragement, laughter, tears, and so much more throughout the years. You have such a fierce tenacity in your activism and such a delicate compassion in your collaboration.

I will never find enough words to thank my company co-founder and best friend Derek Chan. You were the first person to ever believe that I could write anything worth staging. You pushed me to never settle for good enough and always made me feel as though I belonged in a scene that can at times make me feel so small. Thank you my friend, this privilege of being published is one I share with you.

Gratitude to everyone I grew up with in Chetwynd, I carry a piece of you all with me. Thank you to the real Melissa and Candice, I treasure the friendships that we have had since childhood. To the real-life Greg, thank you for everything we have been through together since kindergarten. A best friend like you is an incredible thing to have in life. This play is a tribute to that kind of friendship, one that has survived so much, spanning decades and thousands of kilometres.

To my sister Teresa, thank you for letting me interview you for this play and for taking care of me when Dad got sick. You helped raise me and I am so much better for it. Mom, your unwavering support has meant the world to me. Dad, I miss you every day. Thank you both, for making Chetwynd your home, without that, none of these stories could have happened.

To the love of my life, Jessica, I am eternally grateful to have you along for this ride. You've done so much over the course of writing this play that it can't be measured. I am incredibly lucky to have you as a partner in life. Not only are you an amazing mother to our two beautiful kids but an incredible artist in your own right. I am so thankful for the family we have made together. To Ian and Pat, my other mom and dad, I can't thank you enough for your cheerleading and support.

Thanks to Playwrights Canada Press and the whole team there for this wonderful opportunity. You've been so kind and patient with me as I navigate being published for the first time. Finally big thanks to Deneh'Cho Thompson who shot me a message asking if I was thinking of publishing anything and if he could read a draft. You opened the door to an opportunity I never thought I could have.

Pedro Chamale (he/him) was born and raised on the unceded, ancestral, and traditional territories of the Treaty 8 Nations, including Sikanni, Slavey, Beaver (Dunne-za), Cree, and Saulteau, in Chetwynd, BC. He now lives on the lands of the Qayqayt First Nations, New Westminster, BC. He creates on the unceded and traditional lands of the xʷməθkwəy̓əm (Musqueam), Skwxwú7mesh (Squamish), and Səl̓ílwətaɬ (Tsleil-Waututh) nations colonially known as Vancouver, BC. He completed the acting program at Douglas College and then received his BFA in Theatre Performance from SFU's School for the Contemporary Arts. He went on to form rice & beans theatre with Derek Chan in 2010, where he is currently Artistic Director. Pedro is also a director and performer. He was Artistic Resident at Neworld Theatre in 2014, guest curator of the 2018 rEvolver Festival, and one of the playwrights in the 2019 Playwright's Lab at the Banff Centre. Pedro was part of the second cohort of Banff's Arts and Culture Leadership, is a co-founder of the Canadian Latinx Theatre Artist Coalition, sits on the Latinx Theatre Commons steering committee, and was part of Directors Lab North in 2020. With Derek Chan, Pedro was awarded Simon Fraser University's 2021 Young Alumni Excellence Award for their work with rice & beans theatre. In 2023 Pedro was a nominee for the BC Multicultural and Anti-Racist Breaking Barriers Award, for which he is grateful to be recognized for the work he has done both personally and at rice & beans. You can find out more about Pedro's work at www.pedrochamale.com and www.riceandbeanstheatre.com.